SNeeZe.it

Just Don't Say It, Spray It

David Steel

ISBN: 1479370401
ISBN-13: 9781479370405
CreateSpace, North Charleston, SC

Table of Contents

Preface

Prior to starting Sneeze It, I had been running a company primarily focused on sales and teaching sales management and training. About four years ago, Sneeze It was born in a desire to implement the sales ideas online. These days, companies are finding that using social media for sales is an essential component of their business (one of the main reasons why I wrote this book). But the idea of using social media ("Isn't it just something that kids use?") for purposes of sales did not take off right away.

It's like a bumblebee. If you examine the physics of a bumblebee, so it is said, it really should not be able to fly. Usually someone says something like, "A bumble bee shouldn't be able to fly, but the bumble bee doesn't know it, so it goes on flying anyway." In a similar light, surely social media can't be used for sales. That's just not how it's supposed to work. And yet, as many companies are learning, it does work—and it works rather well. (The bumblebee logo is an important part of Sneeze It for this reason.)

Why does marketing using social media work so well? If you look at the history of sales and marketing before the Internet, the message had to be fairly broad. Even if you targeted a specific audience, that audience was still fairly diverse (i.e., women) because the places where companies advertised (magazines, television, bill boards) were seen by larger audiences.

With social media, these targeted audiences can become extremely specific. If your company wanted to run a marketing campaign targeting women between the ages of 20-29 who have blonde hair, live in the South, wear fingernail polish, and exercise three times a week, you can do that. Instead of casting your net broadly and hoping to catch the right audience, you can immediately find that right audience. With the way social media works, we can take a small audience that is more likely to buy or to be motivated to do something and target them cost effectively. We can go far beyond mass marketing and tie into extremely specific segments of the market.

The other aspect that makes social media sales so effective is the idea of two-way communication. Traditional marketing is a one-way relationship where the brand talks to the consumer, not the consumer to the brand. But if you think about it, sales is all about two-way communication. Social media is that two-way communication, the engagement of the brand and the consumers together, and when done right you build advocates for your brand who tell their friends who tell their friends and so on.

Before you know it, your message has gone viral—meaning that it has spread from one person to another. And that's what Sneeze It is all about—spreading your message from one person to the next in an effective manner. Like a virus that can be spread by a single sneeze, sometimes just one person can be enough to spread something to a much larger group. If you think about it, when someone sneezes, it is loud, stands out, and causes other people around that person to take an action (such as saying "Bless you"). That's what you want your social media marketing to do—spread from one to the next and get other people to take action.

As you read through this book, you'll see that this plan for social media is not as simple as just creating a page on Facebook and posting a message every now and then. You need an action plan, individualized for your specific business, and you need to build a relationship with your consumers.

All of these items take time and understanding of how social media works. This book was written to help you understand how social media can be used for sales and what it is going to take to get your message going viral, to create those sneezes that will spread from one person to the next. All you need is one influential sneezer to take a product from obscurity to being well known.

Whether you are a large company or a small business, this book can help you develop your social media sales plan. The book has been written like a blueprint so that you can actually design a marketing plan yourself. Although you can certainly read straight through the book in a single sitting, I do not recommend that. If you just read through the book without stopping to play around with the concepts on the computer, you do yourself a disservice.

Instead, read a little, digest it, try it out online, come back to the book, experiment some more, read a little more, etc. The book is set up with a number of ideas or questions for you to consider along the way. Take time to answer these questions as you work your way through the book. You're not going to become an expert at social media sales overnight. Learning how to build this community will take time, and I encourage you to start slowly and build a little bit more each day.

If you decide that you cannot devote the necessary time to implement your social media sales plan and perform the daily tasks (such as responding to comments) that are necessary, consider hiring a company such as Sneeze It to manage your social media. But even if you do outsource your social media campaign, you still need to understand what is actually being done for your brand online and how you can help manage that process because nobody knows the brand better than you.

Also, you'll want to revisit your social media plan every so often as social media is a dynamic entity that is constantly changing. You'll need to make sure that what you've set into place is still working six months to a year down the line. And the more you understand what is involved with social media marketing, the more you can help shape that continuing process.

I want to thank my wife and family for being supportive in the times when Sneeze It was just starting out and for making it through the tough times together. I couldn't have done any of this without you.

I'd also like to thank my forum—a group of people who get together once a month to discuss business issues. Our conversations have been tremendously helpful as Sneeze It has grown.

Finally, my team at Sneeze It is such an important part of why we have created something so great. The individuals on the team are all exceptionally smart and have so many creative ideas about how to use social media. By using our own internal social media network, our creative process is shaped by social media, which helps us generate even more ideas. I have discovered that the collaborative effort that goes on when people who are engaged in social media get together is incredible. When you put marketers who know how to use social media together, they go way beyond the original concept. Together we have accomplished so much more than one person could do alone. Thank you for all that you have done and continue to do.

Introduction

"Did you see that video? It went completely viral in a weekend!"

"Viral" is a term commonly used when speaking about online content that has spread at a rampant pace all over the Internet.

- Viral videos
- Viral articles
- Viral tweets

We have all encountered viral online content. What we have to understand is that this viral content doesn't just happen. It is not like a mushroom that just springs up in the darkness and appears like magic the next morning.

Instead, this viral content is often the result of "sneezing." Yes, just like the common flu virus is spread from person to person, a lot of social media material becomes similar to an "epidemic" when people "sneeze" it.

Here is what we mean:

A blog is posted on a website, and someone reads it. That person leaves a comment (one sneeze) and also "Likes" it on Facebook (another sneeze). Other viewers see the comment and also the social media sharing that occurred with that "Like."

Those people share the blog with others in this same way. They make some comments that get others responding as well. Soon this blog post has gone viral, and well, you know the rest of the story.

What works for a blog post, spreading a good idea (or even a not-so-good idea), is also a remarkably effective platform for sales.

Ahhchooo!

This book is about selling products and services in the digital age using social media. Although using social media for sales is certainly a simple idea, it is often too *overly simplified* in the minds of those who want to use it.

Throughout this book we will refer to the item/idea/service that you are selling as "Product XYZ." So you want to sell Product XYZ, and you want to use the "sneeze effect" through channels such as Facebook, Twitter, Pinterest, and other social media to do so.

You begin making blogs, vlogs (video blogs), and all kinds of comments on your various social media accounts but you find little success. A few odd friends or acquaintances "like" or "follow" you, but no leap in sales occurs.

What's going on? Isn't social media the best way to draw attention to Product XYZ and create traffic to your sales website?

It can be, but not in the way just described above. You cannot simply make use of the social networks in an offhand manner and get a lot of desirable results. You need a focused plan and target.

Not having a focus is a major oversight in many people's plans, but this book will help you avoid wasting even one moment of time by giving you a multi-step process for successful sales using social media marketing.

So if you're ready to begin, break out a box of tissues and get ready to learn all about how to do a lot of focused sneezing to get Product XYZ selling right away.

Chapter One

Social Media Today

The techniques we use at Sneeze It, my social media marketing firm, offer a good illustration of why you should understand the classic definition of social media if you are to use it to the fullest extent possible.

I will frequently refer back to the way we do our social media marketing and also recommend that you keep a firm like Sneeze It in mind if you discover that you will be unable to handle social media work in the ways described here.

Why? Social media work is so important to the modern business and sales models that you cannot just "wing it" or ignore it, and you certainly cannot view sales in the traditional way any longer. You need to either become experienced with social media yourself or find someone who is experienced to help you.

What is Social Media?

So what is social media? We can simplify it, such as "Oh, social media is something like Facebook and LinkedIn," but that isn't the best answer because it doesn't really explain anything.

We prefer the following definition, which is posted on numerous sites online:

"Social media refers to the use of web- and mobile-based technologies to turn communication into an interactive dialogue [...using] a group of Internet-based applications that build on the ideological and technological foundations of Web 2.0 and that allow the creation and exchange of user-generated content."

"Interactive dialogue" is a wonderful way to view social media. Not just two people socializing electronically, social media is instead an enormous forum for lots of interaction, discussion, and the sharing of information. It uses much more than text or pages of information as well; social media may be entirely visual, audio, or a combination of both.

This broad expanse of social media means that the demand is heavy for content created by professionals and consumers alike and that the entire world of social media depends upon this mixture of materials or media.

Something to keep in mind is that social media is "user generated," which gives it a level of validity required for consumers to act or at least to be far more motivated than they are by a more traditional advertisement.

Why is that? Let's learn about user-generated content to understand how this works clearly.

User Generated = Marketing Gold

You will discover that social media, and most of the sites relating to it, are often called user generated, meaning that the actual users of these sites have a hand in participating and creating the content. This user-generated content is referred to by business owners, marketing experts, and many others as "marketing gold" for lots of valid reasons.

The top two reasons for this view of user-generated content are

1. Because it is a clear form of Word of Mouth (WOM)

2. Because it is the foundation of all Social Influence Marketing

Before we begin to discuss these two aspects, let's be sure that we fully understand what we mean by user-generated content.

What is WOM?

The traditional website experience is as follows:

1. *Use a search engine to find what you want, need, desire, etc.*

2. *Head to a few of the websites from the search engine results*

3. *Read content created by marketers or advertisers who hope to "pitch" their products, services, etc.*

4. *Make your choice based on this material, which is designed to be very influential and biased.*

When a site is crafted from user-generated content, as is the vast majority of the information on social networks, the experience is different from the above because the content is not created by marketers or advertisers to bias your decision.

Instead, the materials that you read, watch, view, or listen to are created by individuals with no sales agenda. These people are exchanging thoughts, ideas, and opinions and are even using social media just as a form of entertainment.

So the guy who posts the sexy image of the girls he saw in t-shirts with a famous beer logo or the people who post a notice that they are currently at a specific restaurant, store, or tourist attraction are all creating user-generated content. The distinguishing factor here is that they did this "just because" they wanted to share the information about their lives rather than to try to sell something.

They are not directly trying to get their friends or colleagues to buy that beer or to visit those places. Instead, they have created the content to share it and to spread the word about something they like or recommend. This sharing may lead those friends to buy a product or visit a place because of the one who posted it, but that would be an indirect result rather than the desired aim.

They may also be interested in opening a conversation about these postings, but the point is that a dialogue rather than simply an advertisement is being created.

WOM's Significance

We would have to say that social media has more than a single meaning and that modern day "word of mouth" is most certainly one of them.

Consumer studies of all kinds have shown that most shoppers tend to choose products if they come recommended by friends, family, or acquaintances. In 2012, the Global Trust in Advertising Report indicated that 92% of consumers preferred recommendations from family and friends over any other form of advertising.

While these recommendations are not the exact same as social networking or social media, what the studies demonstrate is that the "conversations" or the exchanges of recommendations and opinions often begin with social media. In fact, one study showed that 81% of consumers on Facebook use the site every day, which can get them initially engaged with a product or message.

Stop and think about it: if the "head count" at Facebook is around 950 million people, roughly 750 million are using the site each day. Not only is that an enormous market, but it shows the importance of creating a social media strategy designed around the WOM ideal.

Word of mouth has a few definitions that range from "gossip" to spoken communications that express or report information, opinions, beliefs, facts, etc. from person to person.

What you need to take from any of these definitions is fairly simple: word of mouth is one person telling another person about something.

In the social media model, however, when one person tells another something, it often means that they tell all of their friends through a single message.

For example, you tweet that you are with some friends or colleagues at a restaurant in Seattle, WA. This tweet triggers others to comment if they have been there, heard about it, or want to visit that area. No sale is occurring at the restaurant (beyond the first customer), but a lot of "buzz" has been created around the person who tweeted and the topic of his tweet—the restaurant. This wildfire form of WOM demonstrates why WOM is so appealing as a sales tool.

Generally, people do not give one another opinions or information without a reason. Most often those reasons are one or more of the following:

- Warn someone about a bad product, business, service, etc.
- Encourage someone to try a product, business, service, etc.
- Share an opinion about something when asked for it
- Tell someone something because it is interesting or useful for them to know

This means that those social media recommendations from family, friends, and colleagues that influence around 92% of the consumer market are most often a very valid form of WOM.

What is so beneficial for you is the simple fact that social media and the interactions that it creates are a form of exchange—a form of exchange in which many recommendations or opinions are often expressed. The use of social media is nearly identical to creating valid WOM except it is far more targeted and direct than "organic" WOM.

Key Sources for Online WOM

Consider these places where you can easily find WOM that is more focused than "real world" dialogues:

Review websites. Just stop to consider the user-generated reviews for materials available on Amazon.com, CNET.com, or Edmunds.com. These three sites are very different types of sites, but they encourage clients to leave reviews about the items they have purchased. This review does not benefit the reviewer, but it certainly opens up a dialogue and allows the search and purchase process to become far more informative and interactive. These reviews are definitely WOM because they are personal opinions, but they have that added "kick" because they are very subject-specific websites, with comments provided by enthusiasts and knowledgeable buyers.

Blogs. Blogs are entering a "gray" area because they can be related directly to sales, but they are the epitome of user-generated content. Blogs, or web logs, have been around for a while, and some are coming heavily under the influence of corporations. The "true" blogs still give readers personal opinions and thoughts, and even the corporate blogs tend to have free and open forums for feedback. Thus, they are a trusted form of WOM.

Wikis. Any of the "wiki" sites are collaborative and built entirely from contributed materials. For example, the world's most famous wiki is Wikipedia. The entire community ensures its accuracy and neutrality and you can often find topics "tagged" for improvement or noted for containing questionable information.

Social Media Networks. LinkedIn, Facebook, You Tube, Twitter, Google+, Pinterest and so many more sites allow users to create profiles; enter personal information and interests; share photos, videos, and "likes"; and generally create "launching pads" from which friends or users search for like-minded individuals or those with common interests. Because registered users are allowed to post comments, place images or links, and leave feedback on one another's pages, it is a great approach to WOM.

So in the plainest of terms—

Consider the sneezing that your social media efforts trigger as a form of highly valuable word of mouth.

Next, we need to understand Social Influence Marketing before moving forward.

"Social Influence Marketing"

In a recent survey we conducted with brand managers about social media sales, respondents noted that "traditional top-down branding will become increasingly impotent as social media grows."

In this survey respondents mentioned that consumers will continue to rely on personal networks to learn about products and services and will shape brands almost as much (if not more) as brands themselves.

Thus, we conclude brand management will require greater transparency and a stronger connection to consumers than ever before.

Social Influence Marketing is a system relatively easy to understand and use. How is Social Influence Marketing, or SIM, done? It uses social media sales tactics (of which sneezing is only one facet). What anyone hoping to use social media pages for sales has to remember is that the vast majority of materials on social networks and in social media is user generated.

Thus, the environment is controlled by consumers more than those seeking to use the environment for sales.

Here is what we mean:

Anyone relying on user-generated content has to understand that these sites are in a constant state of change. They have all of the various opinions and materials being shared, which means that the "advertiser" has to become a participant in a dialogue and not a broadcaster speaking to an audience.

You can no longer slap up an advertisement, pay the hosting service to put the ad in relevant traffic, and measure the results. Now you have to decide if you will create a brand page, whether you will allow the public to post comments to it, and how you will use all of the social media networks to discuss the brand.

Are there any risks in this? Absolutely! Consider that you have to give over a huge amount of control to participate in SIM. Rather than creating a campaign and a very defined brand image, the world of user-generated content and SIM means that you are only talking with your viewers and never talking "at them."

They also do a lot of "talking" and you have to work proactively, offensively, and often defensively, too. Why? Because you have to be sure that their talk is not giving your firm a bad name or painting an inaccurate image of it. Opening up to feedback and comments means that negative feedback and comments will most certainly appear, and you must have a strategy to handle these comments to lessen any negativity.

This is where you come into the equation because you will begin a dialogue with your intended clients using all of the different social medial platforms.

Rule #1

Before we look a bit closer at social media, it is imperative to bring up one point that we will re-emphasize many times in this book:

If you are going to engage in social media, be engaged. One of the most substantial blunders business owners make when they attempt to use social media is to use it without engaging in it.

Here is what we mean:

You put up material on every network to get attention, but you only have one hour of each day to follow up with your efforts. This one hour is not going to let you engage in the level necessary to succeed. You miss out on responding to comments, you fall behind on just basic acknowledgments, and you generally present yourself as disinterested (when you are really just unable to handle all of the essential interaction because of poor planning or a lack of time).

Instead, you have just been *reactive* instead of *proactive*. You didn't want to miss the proverbial boat, so you just leapt into all of the various forms of social media at once, but this action is foolhardy because you won't be able to keep up with it.

The key to success with social media is to be able to respond to every single action. Just like we might instinctively say "Gesundheit" or "God bless you" to every sneeze we hear, you *have* to be able to engage and respond on social media as immediately as that.

Fortunately, you can develop an infrastructure that keeps you up to speed with activities such as blog posts or you can work with a firm that creates automatic sharing programs for you. This plan is sure to boost traffic and create "leads."

As we move into this next section about "How Social Media Works," it is vital that you understand the primary rule:

Social media works only if you interact with the audience.

Never forget that definition we provided, that social media is an "interactive dialogue," which means a two-way flow of communication. When you let your audience see that you are not listening (by failing to respond), it might all come to an end right there.

Now that you know the very first rule, you can begin to really explore social media to its fullest degree.

How Social Media Works

There is not just one site or technology that operates social media. The most commonly recognized formats currently include the following:

- Blogs and Forums
- Facebook
- Twitter
- Google+
- LinkedIn
- Pinterest
- Flickr
- YouTube

Whether you know about all of them or not, they form the core structure of modern social media. If you are to do, or cause, any successful sneezing, it will be within this network of networks.

A Network of Networks!

Note that these networks are not all alike. You need to understand how each one is used to be able to choose which ones you will focus on and how you will use that particular network.

Facebook is very diverse and can allow you to make a business "page," post videos, make comments, and include redirect links directly to a website, blog, or landing page (don't worry, we cover all of these topics later).

Twitter gives you a restrictive space to post one compelling statement of 140 characters or less.

LinkedIn allows you to become a professional "expert" across a network of peers in related fields.

Pinterest is entirely visual, as is **Flickr**, but the sites are organized in different ways.

YouTube is all about video content.

Within all of this variety, however, is the world of modern business. You should try to use several of these "languages" to "speak" to the target audience (i.e., you create a great blog *and* embed a video in it, plus you post a Facebook link to the video).

The concept to keep in mind when using social media is that it is the "new" sell, not the classic "hard" sell, and you can go online and find that many business professionals agree.

Why do they agree and what does this mean? They are saying that the old sales models no longer apply because the entire consumer market has changed with the arrival of social media.

Social Media for Business

What do we mean exactly? Let's just run a quick side-by-side comparison to review the old-fashioned sales model against the newer approach:

Old School	New School
Sales representative chases down leads.	Consumer looks for a solution to their wants and needs online.
Sales representative assesses and qualifies leads.	Consumers assess their findings online and narrow down choices based on information discovered (including any social media details).
Appointments are made with potential clients by sales representative or agent.	Consumers explore their possible choices online or participate in initial contact.
Presentation of product or service is performed.	Consumers decide if they want to initiate sale or request trial.
Sales representative answers questions or handles objections.	Consumer contacts company or vendor with any final questions or uses a FAQ at the vendor's website. Often they will use other websites that contain comments and/or complaints.
Sales representative makes the sale or ends interaction based on lack of interest.	Customer makes purchase and begins following vendor through social media (i.e., they become a "Fan" on Facebook or "Follow" on Twitter to keep up to date on sales, specials, news, etc.).
Sales agent now moves on to next lead or candidate.	Consumers make public post or comment about their experience and remain in contact with firm if so desired. They often share vendor information on social media pages, too.

Notice the incredible difference? One side emphasizes the sales representative and the other is consumer oriented.

Though the new model looks a lot like a sort of "DIY" project with the consumer doing the exploring and searching, consumers have shown they prefer this model. They want to do the legwork and initiate contact.

Instead of getting direct mailings, cold calls, and pushy sales tactics, the availability of the Internet and social media lets the consumer control the pace and the level of interaction with the vendor. The option to create "user-generated content" also means that the consumer is controlling the terms, vocabulary, and subject matter, too.

This consumer-driven approach does create some challenges for sales professionals and business owners because it doesn't provide them with a lot of opportunities for the classic "needs assessment" sales method.

This method allows them to thoroughly understand their audience by asking basic questions and then showing (instantly) how they are the solution needed. They reach these conclusions by asking questions such as the following:

What are the consumer's or viewer's needs, wishes, wants?

What do I have as an answer to them?

How do I show them that I have what they need?

Just Like an Interview

Of course, buried in this needs assessment is an "interview" of sorts and a way to get a lot of valuable information, which is the very reason that it has been used for many years in the world of sales.

The new method doesn't mean that you abandon those questions when relying on social media; you still have to have all of those answers, but you don't use them to position a sales statement.

For example, consider this example of the basic needs assessment sales model.

You conduct some market research and discover a strong need for vitamin formulas to address specific health concerns. You create a sales area on your website and trigger a chat box to open when someone begins exploring the page. The sales approach is like this:

Vendor: *I see you've noticed our vitamins. Is there something specific you require?*

Buyer: *I need supplements for a few different health issues.*

Vendor: *We can choose supplements based on broad needs. For instance, these vitamins are good for people with seasonal allergies and sinus conditions, while those are good for people with joint issues. What sort of broader needs do you have?*

Buyer: *I have some digestive issues and a heart condition.*

Vendor: *Well, these products are the most appropriate for you. I would be happy to go over the formulations to clear this up a bit. Do you have a few minutes?*

The seller determined the need, indicated that they did have solutions, and then pointed the buyer toward the solution. In other words, the seller

- Grabbed consumer attention,
- Delivered the message, and
- Gave the Call to Action.

This example shows a way of using the needs assessment model in the modern format. It also offers good evidence of why the needs assessment model was such a success in the "real world" days of shopping and buying. This example, however, is not precisely how you use the details provided by consumers in social media.

While you won't necessarily be guessing about the products or services that potential clients need (after all, you already have a business idea and some general market information), you will have to learn how to position yourself in the direct gaze of possible buyers without making a sales pitch. You are going to show yourself as an answer to a need, but it is different than the old-fashioned approach.

What Social Media Can't Do

We want to remind you that a newer sales model is in effect the moment you begin to consider selling with social media. Your customers will look for you, and your message has to be out there and waiting (along with a good reputation if possible), which means your market research may need to be viewed a bit differently.

For example, your research says that a certain age group is interested in Product XYZ and that a certain geographic area is the strongest market available. Unless you know how to position yourself in social media networks that this specific group views, your efforts will be in vain.

Quite plainly, the one aspect that social media cannot do for you is put you in the ideal locations for immediate sales. Instead, you have to take the time to develop a logical and tactical strategy.

Social media cannot just send out messages to all of the right people. It requires a lot more than that. In later chapters, we look at all of this in much greater detail. For now, however, you do need to consider the old-fashioned needs assessment issue.

Do you know what your customers need, want, or have to hear to consider buying from you? Maybe not. That's okay because needs assessment is a conversation, a conversation you have with customers or potential customers. Social media is the ideal place to start this conversation.

The next step you have to make is to develop a social media strategy that works like a map guiding you toward the ideal clientele. Social media cannot strategize for you. It just doesn't work that way. You have to create your own strategy.

It begins with some simple planning and setting of goals similar to the original sales model but with some unique twists and turns. That is what we cover in the next chapter.

Chapter Two

Setting Social Media Goals

Do you recall Rule #1 from the previous chapter? It put an emphasis on "responsive" use of social media. You have to keep this rule in mind as you begin to formulate plans and make goals.

Just consider the following idea with which many marketing experts agree:

The reason social media marketing efforts fail is that they are simply broadcasting sales messages. This works, to some degree, in advertising because people stumble upon ads with intent to buy. It works to a degree in email marketing efforts too because people requested messages and the vendor has been given a right "to sell" in that context. Most people don't participate in social networks to shop and that means that sales messages feel sort of unwelcome and can be overwhelming in number and very easy to ignore.

The use of the phrase "simply broadcasting sales messages" is something to take note of because it is such an easy habit to fall into. You could dedicate a lot of your time and effort to creating well-phrased sales pitches and then just paste them everywhere and anywhere out on the Internet.

That, however, is a one-way dialogue, and like throwing a dart while blindfolded, you might hit the mark or you might miss the entire wall.

The initial goal you have to establish in your list of "must do" tasks (where social media is concerned) is to begin a dialogue.

Naturally, this presumes that you are accepting one very simple and fundamental idea about this entire issue: *your social media efforts are going to start as a bit of a learning process.*

After all, what is a dialogue? It is a conversation, an exchange, in which people who are mutually interested in the ongoing discussion have relevant ideas to say to one another. It is the classic "give and take."

Dialogue can be a debate, an informational exchange, and even a bit of gossip, but it is important to note that it always means that people are giving and receiving. It means speaking, but anyone successful at social media sales will tell you it takes listening more than anything else.

You already know that responsiveness is your first rule for social media sales, but you cannot respond effectively if you haven't been listening.

Active Listening

Here is what we mean by listening:

You are interacting with someone and realize that you a "glazing over" a bit because you have allowed yourself to become a "passive" listener. You don't really mean to do it, but you are allowing your attention to be divided into bits and pieces and giving the speaker only one smaller bit of your complete attention.

The active listener, on the other hand, takes in all that is being said and is also formulating questions based on their interest in what they hear.

In other words, you are not allowing yourself to be distracted by other thoughts. Staying focused means you are able to fully understand all that is said.

Active listening is tougher than it might sound because

- You cannot apply any judgment to the ideas you are hearing;
- You have to allow the speaker to shape or direct the conversation or exchange;
- You are supposed to be asking questions that expand and forward the dialogue; and
- You have to guide the dialogue in a way that reflects upon the needs, wishes, wants, desires, etc. of the speaker.

When you are able to listen actively, you will notice that the speaker is much more responsive because he or she can tell that you are showing a great level of interest, sincere interest, in what he or she has to say. This level of interest is true in the "real world" as it is in the online world.

Your primary goal is to establish a valuable dialogue, but you have to know the right "opening line," which takes a bit of background knowledge to create.

Speak the Language

Before we focus on this background information, let's also consider one major benefit that comes from listening: you learn the "lingo."

When you do more listening than talking you can begin to recognize and learn the preferred "language" of the speaker or audience.

You can then use this language each time you speak with your intended audience. Just consider the following:

Your Product XYZ is related to solar energy. You decide to create a blog about the financial benefits of this technology. You have determined that it is a good time to begin using the social media connections you have with businesses in small buildings or factories. You know that you have to find a way to speak with this audience that grabs their attention.

Their preferred language is business and not environmentalism. So the "greenhouse gas" and "fossil fuel" conversations that you use with your environmentalist audience won't work. What will? You find that "net metering" and "interconnection" will get their attention because the terms relate to income generated by solar energy.

Now you understand the audience's language and can shape the message to reflect that.

Okay, so how do you listen? That is the beauty of social media: you will listen by getting feedback, comments, and establishing networks. All of these activities generate lots of "talk," and you should be using it to the fullest extent possible (don't worry, we'll cover all of these aspects shortly).

For now, you need to ensure that you make the information relevant and recognizable, and you will you get a lot of mileage out of your initial communications with your social media audiences.

Now, let's begin developing plans for your social media sales.

The Right Tools and Tactics

The smartest folks using social media understand that they cannot use a list of goals in the same way that they might use a checklist.

Instead, these are the people who apply great amounts of patience in their approaches to social media.

Patience is necessary because they know they are laying the groundwork for a successful formula or path that they will eventually be able to use in the broadest ways possible.

For example, successful use of the "sneeze effect" starts with testing and "tweaking" the message. It involves finding out

Whom to contact,

How to speak to them, and

How to get them to buy and remain loyal.

That is a lot to consider, so we suggest that your initial list of goals look like this:

1. Commit to X-number of hours of social media work each day.
2. Develop a content strategy.

In the first chapter, we spoke about needs assessment sales tactics. This tactic is the classic "find out their needs and wants to sell a solution to the audience in question," but we suggest you take it further.

How? Just consider:

You make Product XYZ, right? And you know what needs this product meets.

To develop a market for it through social media requires that you ask yourself some pointed questions. These questions will help you to discover where your most "qualified" traffic can be found.

The Questions to Ask

1. What does the potential audience for Product XYZ want to talk about? Remember that your social media is not direct sales but a method by which you open that dialogue that will create traffic and generate interest.

2. Where are they going to have the largest number of conversations about these issues related to Product XYZ? Did you know that 75% of households in the U.S. use social media on a daily basis? In fact, they spend over six hours per month on the social networks.

   What you have to determine is if your audience is a Facebook crowd, a LinkedIn group that talks about professional issues, blog viewers who appreciate your posts and videos, or the Tweeters who like brief thoughts and lots of options to post feedback.

3. How can you measure results of any conversations that you have with them about Product XYZ? If you use the social media tools properly, you can often track traffic to your website, landing page, etc. This shows you top traffic sources, but you can also turn to Facebook Insights, YouTube analytics, and others.

Clearly, finding the answers to these three questions will show you what your ideal customers want to talk about and where they hang out to do so.

As we already said, however, it takes patience and requires that you commit to a "learning process."

Measure Opportunities

So, which of the social media are likely to generate the best "buzz" for your product or service? This question is not easy to answer, but we can assure you that the best efforts always begin with one idea: keywords.

Yes, I hear the groans of "No, not more keyword discussions!" And this is a pretty fair reaction. After all, anyone involved in any kind of marketing, sales, or Internet work over the past five years has had their lifetime fill of keyword talk.

Keywords are imperative to your success.

This fact means that the development of your list of social media goals and strategies has to now include keyword analysis.

Know What They Want to Hear

Your Product XYZ offers solutions to your potential customers' wants and needs, but the words used to describe it are also a good way to determine the ways that your audience is talking about it on social media.

For example, let's say that Product XYZ is something used by physical and occupational therapists as a way of treating pain. It is, in "techno-speak," an "Anti Pain Erasure Device" (yes, I just made that up).

Now, if you use that phrase as the keyword in your social media efforts, you are probably going to miss out when trying to speak with your potential buyers or brand advocates.

Why? Because they might call it an "APED," an anti-pain machine, or even a therapy device, and if you were to use only the keywords you have chosen, you will miss all of the conversations they are having, which means you miss out on all of the potential buyers.

You have to begin with a good list of terms that you think your specific audience will use. Now, before you panic about the right ways to do this, understand that you can turn to free tools to help you (or you can hire a professional firm such as my Sneeze It, which has a comprehensive understanding of the matter).

Many people use Google AdWords because it is free of charge and shows you the most popular phrases associated with those you are planning to use. Others do hours of research, and many rely on SEO (more on this a bit later) and marketing experts. You can use any of these ways to manage the issue, but manage it you must!

This keyword work is pretty complicated stuff, and many people have a tough time keeping track of the terms that they have used and the results that they have garnered.

This complication is why we always suggest that a "newbie" to sneezing start by sticking to one or two of the social networks instead of attempting to "go wide" and broadcast the message across as many as possible.

In this way, you can begin to see which of the keywords or combinations of keywords generate the most interest and the best general response. You can then use these same phrases in other social media such as blogs.

Some Words on Keywords

Let's just take a moment for an "aside" here because there is a lot to say about keywords, using them, and the *constantly changing nature of search engines*.

Search engines change? Absolutely! In the past few years the world's most popular search engine, Google, issued three separate updates to its secretive "algorithm." These updates are known as the Panda, Penguin, and Venice updates. Each had a different purpose, and they created some immediate effects.

For instance, the Penguin updates caused some websites to really plummet in search engine results. The reason for the drop was because the update was trying to lower the rank of sites with material that was "keyword stuffed" or which featured duplicate content. Panda, on the other hand, had a goal of lowering the rank of pages that provided a poor user experience due to low-quality content.

The Venice update, which received surprisingly little public debate, provides location-specific support. For instance, you might search for "SEO" using the Google engine and would have normally received global results before Venice. Now, the update targets your location and gives you results based on the IP address.

The updates have been done to the algorithms used by the engines, and to understand this clearly, we now have to define algorithm.

The search engines actually use mathematical calculations to create their results. So the first items you see that are not "sponsored" (purchased listings) are those with the best "organic" results.

These results come from many factors and are often due to someone performing SEO or Search Engine Optimization. A bit later we discuss SEO in depth, but for now you should know that it incorporates the text, tags, links, page design and software (search engines do not read all content, including Flash animations), and originality or authority. It uses this data to determine the order in which search engine results will appear on the screen.

The idea to take from this is that most people consider only the first two screens when they conduct a search, with most looking only at the top ten or less! This means that SEO is imperative for a successful website, but it also plays a role in your social media efforts.

You now know that the keywords that you choose will play a part in how you show up on search engines and how possible clients will (or will not) be able to locate you.

The choice of keywords is important in social media too because your customers or audience will also use the terms as they search for your specific product, service, or business.

Keywords can harm you or help you depending upon the ways you use them.

Using Keywords

At this time it is important that we address the issues of "keyword density," and the two types of keywords at use: long tail and short.

Density is something that relates to SEO or search engine optimization, but it also has a lot to do with getting your name in front of your intended audience. It is a word that describes the overall percentage of any text that is taken up by the chosen keywords.

For instance, your Product XYZ is related to solar energy. You want to have some blogs posted to help with social media and SEO, so you compose (or hire a writer) blogs that have 10% keyword content. We can tell you right now that modern search engine algorithms will look at your blogs with a punitive eye.

Why? When you seem to be "stuffing" pages with keywords they are not likely to contain workable, useable, or informative details. Instead, the search engines view your material as low quality, not in compliance with rules, and not as valuable as pages with natural repetition and use of the terms. What percentage are they accepting? You might be shocked to learn that it can be around one or two percent!

So, a 500-word blog about solar energy might contain the chosen keywords less than ten times and will be ranked higher than a competitor who uses those popular words twenty times or more.

Long tail keywords are often described as being words that are targeted by region, but they are more than that. They use three or more words and are a logical and meaningful phrase. They are used when refinement is imperative to success and when getting specific is going to pay off.

For example, Product XYZ is related to shoes, but not just any shoes. The product is an accessory for "rubber soled knee boots." A person searching for the product could use "rubber boots" or "knee boots," but when they are hoping to get only results for what they want, they are likely to type in a combination of words. One "long tail" option would be "rubber soled knee boots."

How do you know which long tail words to use? Research is the only answer. Only by testing and re-testing them can you determine the ideal terms, and you can then use them in many effective materials and ways.

As we have already suggested, you are well advised to "start small" to keep a good hand on the work you are doing, the results, and the analysis of it all. Starting small simply means that you should limit your social media efforts to a few places and a few terms.

Test the Message

By restricting yourself to a few places, you remain on top of what is happening. Remember, you are going to always base each of your decisions on the ability to be immediately responsive to even a single comment, and if you are scattered far and wide it is impossible to do so.

Also, you are far more likely to get the clearest picture of your "demographic" when you use some basic strategies in selecting the few social networks to use as a starting point. We discuss what we mean below.

Step by Step for Message Testing

Create a basic template or model for your ideal clients, including such factors as age and gender as well as location.

Are the buyers of your Product XYZ from a select or "niche" group, or is it a very diverse population that can use the product?

Use all options for free demographic information about the various social media.

For example, doing a basic search for "statistics that break down social media sites by demographics" will generate tons of current data. In an initial search, we were able to find infographics that delivered a tremendous amount of useful data.

Consider whether you are a B2B (business to business) or a B2C (business to consumer) firm.

Why? If you are a primarily professional site offering business products, focusing on LinkedIn may be much better for you than Facebook, etc.

Consider whether you will do better with local efforts or broader ones.

We already looked at the basics on keywords and business size. So ask yourself if you are a small site or business and if you would do better to focus efforts on local attention rather than broader searches.

Create tools that allow you to "listen" for relevant conversations online as well.

At Sneeze It we use a proprietary targeting analysis called the Total Demographic Analysis (TDA) which gathers information from your website and the website of your top competitors.

The data is analyzed and we discover how people find you, what websites they frequent, what social platforms they normally use, and what kinds of word they use when they chat online because in today's world of connected customers, it's important to have a sharper view of what a typical "customer" looks like, where they congregate online, how they make decisions, and what would motivate them to choose your company over another.

Although not everyone has this type of tool at their disposal, ways to piece this data together using some free online products such as Google Alerts and keyword tool are available.

For example, determine the terms that people use to find your products and services using Google's Keyword Tool and create a Google search for specific news, tweets, terms, etc. Google Alerts can notify you whenever new entries appear. Use RSS subscriptions to follow blogs and track your subjects.

Take all of this information and compare it to the template you have made of your ideal customer(s).

Does everything seem to match? Are you getting attention from the groups that are your most likely buyers? Using this method should show you where to begin your social media efforts and what keywords are the most effective.

You can then create your first "test" messages.

After the First Steps

Just think, by this point you will be able to understand what demographics apply to the people who you want talking about Product XYZ.

You also understand where the most likely places to create and enter into dialogues with them are found.

Lastly, you understand the words that they are using to discuss your product or service, and also the phrases that are associated with it.

Go ahead now and write a brief statement that you think will get a few sneezes. Keep in mind that the content has to be great and that you are trying to set the stage for a trusted relationship between you and the audience. Don't toss out one of those "hey you!" sales messages that get attention but inspire no follow up or which are just blatant pitches.

Instead, create a test message that includes quality information and proves that you are worthy of the audiences' attention. Most of the time it means you are giving away information to attract their attention.

Don't worry—you get a lot for giving away all kinds of materials.

Immediate Rewards

What do you get? Well, if you give away valuable content and information while social networking, you are going to exceed the initial expectations of most of your viewers. How? Your audience will rarely expect "something for nothing" and will know that it will often require a commitment to get anything from you.

Because you have opted to use social media, however, you can create useful and relevant content that they have free access to merely for interacting with you.

Of course, most people using social media for sales will give something away as a sort of bait. This technique is very broad rather than a targeted one.

The following example explains how this works:

If Product XYZ is something related to fitness and you create a free eBook about Physical Fitness Basics *for those who "Like" your Facebook page, you will get a lot of diverse traffic. But what if your product is about a specific type of approach to fitness, such as core training? You would be ahead of the competition if you created some free materials that taught innovative core techniques. For example, the* Five Best Core Moves for Everyone *eBook would get you far more targeted attention.*

Fortunately, if you use our steps for success, by the time you begin to test messages, you already understand what your audience wants to see and hear. And while most businesses are giving away information, you will have done the research that shows you exactly how to exceed any offers from your competition and give the audience what it needs and wants.

While you are giving it all away, however, you are also engaging with your prospective audience.

How? You are asking them to tell you information in return—information about their preferences, their interests, and other factors that standard demographic statistics cannot supply. They don't often realize that you are asking for the information. Just by responding to one of your social media messages, they are indicating something of value to you.

Just remember our example from above:

You decide that Facebook is the most likely place to begin. You create a Facebook page for Product XYZ, and you oblige your potential buyers to become a fan of the page to get the free information. This "socializes" the content and opens everything up to a much wider viewing audience.

Just consider that a new potential customer does as requested and clicks the "Like" button for it. Suddenly, all of their friends with the same wishes, goals, needs, etc. see that this person "Likes Product XYZ." Now, a very targeted audience is going to head to that page to see what it is all about.

Your Facebook analytics will give you a lot of information about those using this link to the Facebook page, and if you have also put links back to your home page or landing page, Google Analytics can help you understand if you have succeeded or not. (Never fear, all of the measuring and analysis is looked at in great detail in subsequent chapters)

Why use analytics if you have developed an effective social media campaign? Because you cannot ever just "know" what to do.

The world of social media is in constant "flux" because it is full of consumer-generated content.

Never forget that there is very little that is "static" about social media. The products that are the hottest around today will be off the proverbial radar next week, but it is still the job of the seller, business owner, organization, etc. to use social media to keep up with this information.

Keeping up takes planning, listening, responding, and measuring the results to work properly.

Don't Believe Everything You See

Before we move on into a more in-depth conversation about attracting an audience, we want to mention the fact that you cannot believe everything that you see. At least, you cannot believe everything right away.

Remember that we put an emphasis on patience a bit earlier? This entire testing process and building of a list of media goals are meant to be a learning process. You cannot rush this process because you will end up with weak or flawed data.

For instance, maybe Twitter was not the ideal place for you to begin developing a social media strategy, but then again you might have to let it evolve a bit more before deciding.

Perhaps you would have done far better to focus your efforts on Facebook or LinkedIn instead?

Maybe Pinterest would have been more effective than YouTube?

Give these questions a bit of time before making decisions. We would say that a full month of effort with one social network is the absolute minimum before you can understand if your tactics are succeeding or not.

Also, keep the realities of statistics in mind. According to one group of statistics, more people have smartphones than toothbrushes. Does that seem on the mark? No, and that means that you have to be a bit skeptical about all of the facts and figures you might run across.

The key is to use patience and the facts you get from your own experiences and research. While pre-existing statistics may be handy, you have to discover your audience from your precise location and begin using your knowledge to develop your marketing plans.

Another Line of Approach

Of course we have not yet mentioned one of the most obvious ways to develop your tactics, and that is by interacting right now!

We already said that social networks have to be developed, but it can start with you, and it can start immediately.

For example, go online right now and commit yourself to finding, following, "Friending," or "Connecting" with at least 20 to 50 people in your industry or who are talking about issues related to your product; they can even be existing customers.

Why? You will have to realize that if you ask for some sort of networking connection with those 50 people, most of them will respond and also connect back to you. That means around 20 people might be following you by this evening. Remember it not just the 20 people you would be connected to but all the people in their network as well.

This is the foundation of building a community or networking: reaching out to like-minded individuals and establishing ongoing relationships.

The key is to be sure that those who are following you are going to be relevant sources of traffic or good members of your desired audience. Don't just add friends or old colleagues because these may not generate any valuable attention. Choose people who can help you develop a larger network of those related directly to your field, product, industry, etc. Keep your personal social connections separate and if they happen to find your business social media site simply point them to your personal social sites.

Don't overlook the fact that you already have some regular contacts as well. Whether you have been involved in social media or not, you have an email list, customers, vendors, and even some strategic partners.

You have a core group of acquaintances that you can also view as your earliest social media network. Even if they are "evangelists" that spread the word by "sneezing" or sharing data, it is going to all add up to interest, traffic, and sales.

Have an email list? Why not send a message letting them know that they can "Like" your Facebook page, "Follow" you on Twitter, or "Connect" with you immediately on LinkedIn. You can use this with Pinterest and Google+ too. The more ways you connect with someone the better, keeping in mind each person may choose to communicate differently even though they are on multiple sites.

These are all great subjects on which to test your messages and keywords as well as the tactics you are thinking of using.

The First Official "To Do" List

You really do have to test the waters, but if you do so according to an organized plan, you get solid results. This test is just not something that can be done overnight. Basically, it boils down to establishing a list of goals and sticking with it.

So far, you should have the following goals for yourself and your social media efforts:

1. Commit to X-number of hours of social media work each day (start small).

2. Develop a content strategy:

    a. Keyword analysis

    b. Demographic harvesting

    c. Define yourself

1. Create a template for your ideal client

2. Choose one or two sites to use for initial social media efforts

3. Test the message using keywords

    a. Give it away: be sure you are giving away top-of-the-line information

    b. Gather it in: accept the details that your audience offers about itself and its interests

    c. Use a clinical eye to measure results

    d. Assess and analyze everything

Of course, as time passes that list of your goals may shift because you will have found a very clear path to success.

For instance, some of the items on this list will disappear once you have hit on the right keywords and actually established a social media presence.

Your Sub-Set of "To Do" Items

So where does that leave us? It means that a secondary set of social media goals might more accurately include the following:

1. Get the attention of your market
2. Earn their respect for you and your knowledge
3. Motivate them to like the product
4. Engage your audience
5. Develop ongoing sales

"Easy," you might say, "but up to this point it has all been a bit theoretical. What about the meat and bones? The how to?"

The next few chapters really pick apart all of the broader points we have covered up to now and will really help you understand how to get started.

Don't discard one of the lists above in favor of another because both sets of tasks are going to prove vital to your success.

Do develop content strategy, but also think beyond that issue. This will help you develop the most workable social media sales tactics possible.

Now, let's begin looking at the "essentials" in greater depth, beginning with "attraction."

Chapter Three

Locating Customers

You understand that you can use social media to get people talking. You also understand that you can use Facebook or LinkedIn to "make the sale," but we haven't really explained how all of that actually works.

In this chapter, we are going to look specifically at the issue of "attracting traffic" to make the sale. Remember, however, that you will need to have tackled some of the tasks from Chapter Two if you want to move forward.

At the very least, you need to identify the keywords that your audience will use when they search for your type of product or service. Once you have these, you do have the "keys" to unlocking sales potential through social media activities because you know the words that your audience uses to express their attraction, interest, and even their intent.

Understanding Attraction in the World of Social Media

Right, so what is attraction? We have to see attraction in a few ways if we are to understand how to use it for social media success.

Consider the following definitions:

A thing or place that draws visitors by providing something of interest or pleasure.

A quality or feature of something or someone that evokes interest, liking, or desire.

A force under the influence of which objects tend to move toward each other.

If we were strictly talking about sales we might be discussing "Features and Benefits." However, we need to go beyond that to what those "Features and Benefits" mean to our customers.

That all sounds great and really does apply to social media and sales. Just consider what we mean:

- *We definitely want to use attraction for improved sales.*
- *We will seek to draw visitors to a website, to evoke their interest, and to bring our product together with the audience that needs it.*
- *We also want to consider the simple act of attracting appropriate traffic to our website through the social media pages.*

If you are not clear about the meaning of "appropriate traffic," just think of it as an endless line of shoppers who have already shown an interest in what we are selling at our site.

You don't want people looking for hammers to be directed to your ballet dancing supply shop. You want to find a way to draw visitors to your social media pages who are going to have a specific interest in what you are hoping to sell or promote. Drawing visitors is not the same as advertising, however, and we are going to persistently remind you of this difference.

For example, a friend of yours on Facebook sees that you have recently "Liked" a brand of shoes. They click the link on their Timeline and head to that shoe company's page and then on to their website.

This is "qualified traffic" because it is someone who already has a serious intention to buy as he makes his way to the site. This person is a type of traffic that has passed the necessary qualifications to move into the actual content of the site but who has done so because he or she relied on WOM and details found on social media and blogs. We affectionately call this type of traffic Warm Traffic.

You want to make sure that the traffic you are generating through social media has that same strong intention and understanding of where they are headed when using any of the links you have posted. This focus most often requires strong and clear branding.

Branding Your Social Media

It doesn't take a social media mastermind to properly "brand" their profiles.

For instance, you can just create some of the following:

- A brand name YouTube channel
- A business page on Facebook
- A custom Twitter background for your page at Twitter
- A Facebook landing page
- A very detailed history or profile for LinkedIn

Any of the social media can be heavily branded, including Pinterest, if that is what you decide to use.

The branding is so important for two reasons:

It allows you to really distinguish yourself from the rest of the crowd.

It helps to create a level of credibility that leads to brand trust.

Of course, you can logo everything to the proverbial hilt and still not give yourself much credibility because you might be spreading yourself too thin and remaining a bit non-responsive. You might also lack consistency, which is a big "red warning light" to potential buyers. You may just come across as a flashy and valueless brand.

Here is what we mean:

You might sink a ton of your effort and energy into creating a really killer YouTube video. You get a surge of interest from it, but then you don't post another video for weeks or months down the road.

You don't respond to comments and you don't share the video across all of your social media pages. Guess what? No one is watching you anymore.

One tweet, profile update, expert commentary, or blog post is never enough to generate respect, credibility, and ongoing traffic.

You need to become an expert and demonstrate that this material is going to just keep on coming for a long time. A great way to do that is to post regular videos or blogs, and to be sure that they are headed back to your website through links, shares, back links, and more.

When you decide to commit to the creation of social media postings that contain links back to the site, it really keeps you "honest," so to speak. You cannot disappear, ignore comments, or remain out of touch if you are updating the website and creating new links.

Remember that your goal is not *to develop the world's biggest Facebook following or the longest list of professional connections.*

Your goal is to open a dialogue with those interested in your product or service. You will use social media to create a familiar and branded presence on the sites where your qualified traffic already hangs out.

Here, as Shakespeare might say, is the "rub." Why? Because you cannot begin broadcasting on Facebook, Pinterest, Twitter, and YouTube and expect people to just find you. Even with the best branding efforts this strategy will not work.

You cannot expect *anyone* to find you, let alone some very targeted traffic, unless you have done the work that ensures you are seen.

This realization is often the reason that a lot of businesses begin with very precise blogs that use the most appropriate keywords. This approach is a simple and straightforward way to direct traffic to social media and vice versa.

Let's go back to that killer video into which you put tons of effort. You could easily have it transcribed and used in a blog post. You could take snippets of it for tweets and posts on Facebook. Furthermore, stills from the video can be used on Pinterest and Flickr. Use one piece of content until nothing is left.

Blog, Blog, and More Blogs

A blog (actually a web log) is a public, online journal where people can document their experiences, post their opinions, or promote their own ideas/products/services. A blog is usually written by one person and focuses on a chosen theme or subject (i.e., a blogger about clothing, food, health, etc.)

Blogging has exploded—everyone seems to have something to say or to sell. A blog is, however, a good way to also engage or attract your audience because you can blog "around" your keywords and create amazing results.

For example, let's say that Product XYZ has a blog link or tab on the website. This blog is going to be updated at least once each week. It will contain news, interesting material related to the purpose or industry of the product, and maybe also guest blogs full of relevant material. It should also have images, videos, and links to related sites or material.

The purpose of this blog is to establish yourself as an expert through the free and reliable information posted in the blog, but it also gives you a lot of options:

- You can embed a link to your newest blogs on Facebook
- You can Tweet about the new blog on Twitter
- You can post links to blogs on LinkedIn
- You can embed links in some of the related images on your Pinterest boards
- You can fill the blog with images and "metadata"
- You can announce any videos through social media
- You can use all of the above for enhanced SEO

SEO In-Depth

What is SEO? We spoke of it in a previous chapter, and we still don't want to get too involved with the issue of SEO here. We are not trying to show you the best ways of having a website at the top of search engine results; we want to show you how to use social media to generate traffic and sales. Still, we do need to discuss SEO briefly.

SEO means "search engine optimization" and is a whole collection of activities that will result in a website (or some of its pages) ending up in the top of the search engine results. The most common tactics performed for page or site optimization include the following:

Page optimization. A website's pages are assessed for their design, use of text and titles that feature keywords, and layout that ensures search "bots" can read the entire page properly (such as keywords in tags, metadata, and more).

Links. Incoming links from URLs shared at social media sites, on other blogs, in articles, and in other valid areas are considered beneficial; links from guest blogs and some online content are also good; and links from valid directories are good as well.

Social Media. By creating libraries of podcasts, videos, and active social media pages, you are going to generate buzz and traffic.

What comes from SEO? Someone who uses a good search engine and the keywords you have employed will find your materials right away. This is, clearly, good for sales, but it also establishes an immediate positive reputation that gives you a huge amount of credibility.

After all, if you were searching for information and found a step-by-step video or a few articles from a very authoritative voice (along with lots of comments and social media interaction) wouldn't you think of the owner of the materials as an "authority"? That is precisely why you want to consider SEO.

SEO In Action

Here is a quick illustration:

- *You have a website that sells something. You create a social media strategy that identifies and uses the strongest keywords.*
- *In addition to using those keywords in your social media efforts, you also use them in your blogs.*

- *Links to the blogs are posted to social media to help drive traffic to the blog.*
- *In the blog, you embed some videos, which are very useful because they "pitch" the product or service and give you great results in Google search results.*
- *The use of the keywords in the blogs, videos, social media, and the relevant web pages all help to constantly keep you at the top of the search engine results pages (also called SERPs for short).*
- *Your site and associated materials are SEO—search engine optimized.*

It sounds so easy, doesn't it? The fact of the matter is that it is one of the trickiest tasks to do.

In addition to finding the right keywords, you have to

Remain aware of the different updates in the search engine algorithms,

Be sure that you use keywords effectively, and

Constantly update all of the content you post on the website and in any social media settings.

This adds up to one basic and unavoidable fact—content is now, and seems like it will always be, the "king" of online success.

While it may be an issue strongly associated with SEO, you have to understand that your consistency in posting to social media and your responsiveness to your audience are all considered to be updated content. This idea means that you must commit yourself to constant effort with social media for it to pay off.

Content is King

What exactly is the content in terms of social media, blogs, and websites? Content is a lot more than the "body" of the blog or the page on the site.

Content includes, but is not limited, to the following:

- SEO blogs and traditional blog content
- SEO articles and regular articles posted to social media platforms and article directories
- Wall posts on Facebook
- Interactions on Facebook
- Tweets
- Twitter interactions
- Google+ posts
- Google+ interactions
- Profiles on sites such as LinkedIn
- Pinterest Boards
- Photos (including those on Flickr)
- YouTube videos
- Tags, titles, and identifying labels on all content listed above

You might scratch your head in wonder over so many items, but we give you the list to demonstrate the need to be sure that everything you compose is done with thought and care. Even the title or tags of videos can be optimized for SEO purposes.

How so?

Let's say that Product XYZ has a website and a blog. In the blog are video "how tos" that give instructions for projects relating to the use of the product. While you will use the keywords linked to the content of the videos in areas such as blog posts, guest blogs, and articles, you also have to incorporate them into areas such as metadata.

These are the HTML tags, titles, keyword tags, descriptions, headings, and anything else that a search engine might read and index.

Creating metadata ensures the greatest results because the information is always pointing back to your website or blog, which establishes you as an authority. It results in good SEO, but it also positions you as a key figure in the industry or business because of the knowledge base you have established.

The important idea to take from all of the above is that your content in social media sites can get you a "Like," "Tweet," or comment that is the same as a traditional "lead," yet this person may not have even seen your website yet!

Without any use of sales jargon or "buy now" tactics, you have gotten them engaged through the social media channels. And now you can "nurture" the relationship without much effort and without forcing them to a landing page or sales page on your website.

Just keep in mind that not all visitors are ready to become leads. Many consumers understand the classic sales cycles and hope to avoid them. When you give them the chance to subscribe to a blog, follow your Tweets, etc., you allow them to take a more passive position, yet you don't lose the opportunity to eventually make the sale.

During this time your tracking and analysis are going to pay off at profound levels.

Why? Because you will begin to see where the most "leads" are coming from and whether or not they are "converting" to actual sales.

Lead Generation

Let's start small here: a "lead," in the classic sense, is defined as follows:

"A sales lead is an individual who has not only the authority, but the interest to purchase a product or service."

In other words, a lead is actually a "potential customer."

The ways of gathering leads are many and have changed pretty radically with the advent of the Internet. The point of your social media efforts will be to attract "leads" and to eventually "convert" them into customers.

Fortunately, attracting and converting leads is something that millions of business professionals are doing with social media, which has created a lot of tools that allow you to review the traffic associated with your efforts.

You can use Google Analytics to see which keywords sent people to your site or to see if Facebook or a search engine result was responsible for "clicks," among other bits of information.

The main point to take from this information is where the largest amount of "converted" traffic is coming from. This information is going to show you your most effective lead-generation tactics.

Sources for Trackable Leads through Social Media

So how is it done? The most direct and effective sources we can provide for generating attention include the following:

SEO Websites and Blogs

Be sure that the content gives great search engine results.

Blogging

Use your keywords and research to generate effective, relevant, and fresh materials. Disperse new materials through social channels.

Common Interest Groups

Social media is always, and we mean always, *developed around common interests. This fact means you can leverage the presence of these pre-existing communities for your sales goals. The most direct way of accomplishing this goal is to become a member of these groups and then present new information, news, energy, comments, etc. You can use search features on any social media sites to seek out common interests, keywords, etc.*

Targeted Content

Yes, we already covered targeted content, but let's just put together a few of the puzzle pieces here.

You have some pre-existing contacts that you can use to begin doing social media campaigns. Now, you have started to follow others operating in related industries. You also have a good idea of what other blogs, sites, and social networks are "saying" about your industry, product, or service.

So, how can you roll these factors into content that generates leads? We suggest the following:

Giving good stuff. *Free eBooks, downloadable seminars, whitepapers, newsletters, and other "goodies" will ensure that people respond to your well-informed offers. Something that is* *very popular right now is the "infographic," and allowing free downloads and easy sharing is a great tactic.*

Giving an open platform. *Host an online event that allows experts to interact during a fixed period of time around a specific subject. Be sure to record it and convert it into a whitepaper, eBook, podcast, or animated video.*

Hosting a contest. *Nothing gets qualified leads running to your site faster than a great deal or prize. You can create monthly deals, promotional offers, specials, and even some sort of sweepstakes for your viewers to join. Just think about the opportunities for images, ideas, and so much more: it is a treasure trove of information about your demographic.*

Advertising

You may find that "pay per click," or PPC, ads are a good way to drive traffic to your site. These ads are not part of social media but can be linked closely to your social media keywords and efforts. You might also elect to buy ad space directly on the social media sites, such as Facebook's advertising areas.

Yes, that is a long list, but you don't have to do it all. Just pick and choose those ideas that seem the best fit for your audience.

You can also work with a knowledgeable consultant to help you determine the most appropriate steps. The consultant can work alongside you to develop a social media strategy and can even do a lot of the work for you.

Keep in mind that many businesses see a huge spike in conversions when using social media.

How much of a spike? Upwards of 400% is the norm. You can use it to promote content on a blog or website and instantly generate traffic, but you can also use social media to nurture your audience, which helps tremendously with eventual conversions and the creation of trust and credibility.

For example, a professional "coach" can find tremendous success by creating a Facebook business page and posting motivating, self-affirming, or generally appealing images and quotes. They may not generate sales from this page, but they do position themselves as a credible and valid professional. This tactic then pays off with eventual conversions and all kinds of "sharing" within networks.

Everything really seems to "take off" for those who know how to both attract and engage their audience. Engaging and getting your audience talking is what we cover next.

Chapter Four

Engage Clients

Engaging clients might also be called "maximizing your content discovery." Why? To get people really buzzing, or sneezing, you have to have the kind of material that immediately engages their interest and also makes them want to tell others about it. And you have to produce a lot of it.

Let's never forget that the "word of mouth" factor is a huge issue in sales and that social media is the newest method of word of mouth, i.e., one friend recommends something to another (by clicking "Like," tweeting, etc.), which creates consumer engagement.

The General Order of Engaging Clients

Engaging clients, however, is all part of a process. A few recognizable phases to this process include the following:

1. Creating the right sort of content and ensuring that the desired audience sees it

2. Creating this content on a frequent and regular basis

3. Enabling the sharing of this content freely and broadly

4. Monitoring the results

Within this process you have many opportunities to establish bonds of trust that ensure your clients remain interested in what you have to say and also that they continue to buy and to use word of mouth to tell others.

This process might be through the use of a social "thank you page" (more on this later) or by calling out frequent "sharers" on pages such as Twitter or Facebook to acknowledge them. It is also accomplished through the creation of a lot of material. For example, a blogger who posts a new blog once a week will see less increase in their traffic than the blogger who posts at least twice each week.

Why is this? The more SEO and targeted content that you create, the more the search engines can index your pages and help people to find you. The more of this material that you share through your social media channels, the more opportunities are presented for people to "click through" to your website.

Just consider that the average "shelf life" of a social media link is only three hours.

Yes, you post a blog and send out an alert about it on Twitter and Facebook, but in the next three hours or so that link loses its potency. By the next day it is as if that link were never created at all because it has become "yesterday's news feed."

So if you want to engage an audience, be sure that you are sending out enough high-quality material on a regular basis.

NOTE: You don't want to become one of "those" social media users, posting dozens of items each day, and end up being hidden or even deleted. Aim for two to three items each week, and it is likely that you can keep your audiences' attention. And keep in mind that you have to constantly respond to the reactions from your posts, and if you are overdoing it, you are not likely to be able to keep up with it.

Understanding Retention in the World of Social Media

"Wait," you might say, "why do I have to *retain* an audience if I have already made a conversion or a sale?"

This question initially seems valid, but we are *not* focused on the sales end right now.

We are focused on creating a strong audience through social media and then retaining this audience to continually sell your products, services, and ideas over and over again.

So if you want to retain your audience, you have to engage with them through social media and you have to do so as if they really were "friends" and not clients. We are not saying you have to share your life's darkest secrets but instead mean that you have to work at the relationship and remain in touch to the fullest degree possible.

Again, you may ask "why?" The answer, as you will learn in later chapters, is that you can establish brand "evangelists" or brand advocates who are constantly showing their appreciation by sharing and promoting you, even if they are not spending dollars on you.

Having advocates is very valuable because it is the best way to constantly enlarge your social media network, generate leads, and make sales.

Tactics for Keeping in Touch

Remember that we have already mentioned some of the primary ways of keeping in touch, including the following:

Networking

You may be the shyest person on the planet, but it is simple to network via the Internet. Make friends and connections, become a fan, and follow people who are directly related to your industry or area of expertise (7 or 8 times out of 10 they will follow you back). This network is going to become your foundational market and one of the best ways to get high-quality leads or word of mouth.

Avoiding the Direct Sell

We have already considered the “new” sales model and learned that it is consumer driven and motivated (i.e., they look for you and not the reverse). If you dash into the middle of the social networks with all kinds of clear sales messages, you will fail. Instead, develop a relationship that establishes trust and credibility, and you’ll see much better results.

Positioning Yourself as an Expert

Because you will commit to the creation of excellent content (including blogs, guest blogs, articles, web content, and interesting posts, among others) you can begin to establish yourself as a very knowledgeable expert. Even if you just tweet a great “factoid” you are showing that you know your stuff, and that keeps you in their mind when they think of Product XYZ.

Interacting—ALWAYS!

Never tell yourself that it is okay to skip replying to a single direct comment or post. Whether you just type in a quick "Thank you" or a full-fledged comment, always show that you are listening and responding. Clients and potential customers love to see that they matter, even if they haven't spent one cent on your product or service.

Giving Them Things

The old adage "givers gain" is especially true when using social media to sell. So don't just give away information in your content, try to actually give good items away from time to time. Like what? You can have a great whitepaper, a good article, an infographic, even an eBook that will be beneficial. Such giveaways also help drastically with social media efforts because you can always announce them in connection to a blog or article you want to use to create traffic and good SEO results.

Secondary Tactics for Engagement

How else do you retain your audience? You have to keep in mind that most consumers are used to being "talked at" or "talked to." You can really turn the tables on the competition by speaking "with" your audience. Speaking with your audience erases the sales pressure and sales messages.

We suggest the following approaches:

Slowly turn up the heat. Marketers call it "boiling the frog," and here's why: supposedly you can put a frog into hot water and it jumps right out, but if you put it into cool water and slowly turn up the heat it will just remain in place. That is a pretty terrible idea, but it is the way that marketers and social media success stories operate. They don't slam their new arrivals with a "Hey, look at what I have here, why don't you buy it" message. Instead, they give them a warm welcome and a few "did you know" items over the course of weeks or months to stir up interest and continue a pressure-free engagement. Only then do they begin to shift to the theme of the messages to "needs answered" through a purchase.

Speak with a personal voice. If you want to engage people and retain their attention, don't use sales speak or formal language. Instead, develop a clear voice and one with which your audience can relate. For example, spend some time and thought in customizing each message used to attract attention on social media pages.

Think like a window shopper. People are using social media and the Internet to find the products or services they want. Try to put yourself in their position and view your messages and your content through that sort of "lens." This lens can often train you to create the most "buzzy" content imaginable.

Naturally, this last suggestion requires a bit more information. After all, what is "buzzy" content but viral content? And this entire book is about creating the kind of viral messages that you need to attract, engage, and retain your clients.

Most people want to be affiliated with the cool and trendy long before a wider base of people who knows them. This concept means you have to establish yourself as a source of good buzz even before you are a true "hit" online.

Creating a Buzz

Here is something to remember: when we say you want to create a buzz it never means creating controversy. Sure, that might get attention, but it is short term and pretty destructive.

Instead, what we mean is that you will do something that traditional sales models tell you to avoid at all costs: you will send your traffic away from its current location, usually away from your social media page.

How does this create buzz? The approach that we use keeps you at the top of a viewer's thoughts and establishes nearly permanent lines of communication.

After all, if you're out there selling on the Internet, you have a lot of competitors, and your potential buyers are always going to see the messages from these competitors. Thus, a way to compete and overcome the competition is to be as viewable as they are but to give very useful information.

To keep ahead of the game we recommend that you give them access to all of your social media options from your website home page, even though this initially sends them "off site" to register.

Here is a simple illustration of our point:

A potential client arrives at your home page, landing page, or some other page on your website. It may be through a shared link, a PPC ad, or some other tactic. The point is that they are at the well-designed page and reading your intended message. That is a single encounter, and the trick is to keep them available and to continue to engage with them after this initial "meeting."

How do you do it? You make sure that they can subscribe to all of your social media directly through that page. Give them a chance to "Like" you on Facebook, to Follow you on Twitter, to subscribe to your blog or RSS feeds, to watch you on Pinterest, and to subscribe to your YouTube channel from that page (as well as any other social media you are using).

Yes, you are sending them away from the page you worked so hard to get them to, but you are then opening a door to a "relationship" and not a "one-time encounter."

You are also giving yourself the prime opportunity to interact with clients, listen to what they have to say, and provide them with solutions to their needs (which is huge).

The goal here is for you to offer such compelling information "value" to a visitor as to have them relinquish their anonymity, allowing you to create a relationship.

Meet the Widget

The most common way to introduce all of your social media options is through the widget.

Basically, a widget is an "app" or application that is installed on a web page by the "end user" (in other words, it is an application that you choose to install on your different pages).

You need to obtain the appropriate "code" to add all of your social media icons to your website. This icon is a very recognizable symbol and cue that lets them (with a single click) join the social media network indicated.

They are also an ideal way to advertise that you are an active member of that particular social network, which is a substantial issue.

Why? When a modern business has no social media presence it tends to actually confuse audience members. Consumers today demand the option of finding their favorite companies not only on their official websites but also in the worlds of Facebook, Twitter, etc.

Using a widget code creator is an easy method of ensuring you announce all of your online locations. You can handle this as a DIY venture, but a social media marketing firm can help you to get and use the codes. Currently, they are available for the following social media sites:

- ActiveRain
- Blogger
- Delicious
- Digg
- Facebook
- Google+
- LinkedIn
- Market Snapshot
- MySpace
- Pinterest
- Posterous
- Reddit
- RSS Feed
- StumbleUpon
- Twitter
- WordPress
- YouTube
- Many others

By making it easy for someone to engage in your social media pages directly from a home page or landing page, you are maximizing your chances at retention. Of course, you do have to be certain that you are providing valuable material to your clients through any and all social media communication.

Why? If you become an annoying, pointless broadcaster of sales pitches, you are just a click away from a permanent break with your audience. They can un-follow, unsubscribe, de-friend, etc., and you will not (for the most part) be able to get them back. You might also set the stage for negative word of mouth, and that is just as horrible.

What, Where, and Why

We want to show you a few ways that social media works in your favor and establishes you as a highly trusted resource.

Example 1

You learned a bit earlier that social media links have expiration dates, but you also know that you cannot continually churn out top quality material on a daily basis—when would you do your actual job?

Instead, you have come to learn that

- You can publish two really good blog posts each month,
- You can make fun and informative videos to insert into these blogs, and
- You can create brief whitepapers about the subject of the blog and even ask a guest blogger or industry expert to post comments.

Guess what? You now have several reasons to communicate with your social media audience about those two high-quality blog posts. For example,

1. *You write a blog and post it. This post sends out messages to anyone who has subscribed to your blog.*

2. *You post a link about the newest blog on Facebook, Twitter, LinkedIn, etc. This link goes to all of your social media contacts.*

3. *A week later you can post the link to the video on all of the same social media sites. It looks like brand new material, but is just the same blog.*

4. *Sometime later, you can post an announcement about the white paper. This announcement goes to social media contacts and provides them with added value on top of the details in the blog and video.*

5. *Finally, if you can have a guest blogger or some sort of forum, you can then announce that on the social media networks and use them to follow up. This point is Example 2.*

Example 2

Engaging the audience and retaining their attention begins when you find ways to enrich their experiences. Enrichment is done by having website content different from that of the social media pages.

For instance, take a look at the following example:

1. *You create some sort of online gathering or event and get your social media contacts to subscribe or attend.*

2. *You then thank each professional presenter through your social media pages. For instance, a status update that thanks the presenter and includes a link to the presenter's website is an effective way to engage the audience's attention and use the materials at hand.*

3. *You include a link to a video or other downloadable version of the presentation or post one at a later date.*

4. *You use the methods from Example 1 to continually communicate about the issue to prolong the expiration date/time of it as a viable subject for social media interaction and discussion.*

Yes, in both examples, you are sending your viewers to places other than sales pages or your website, but you are giving them a lot of value for their participation. This interaction goes a long way in retaining them as potential clients, converted clients, and active audience members. When they are very enthusiastic about your "stuff," they also become brand evangelists in this way.

Example 3

Of course, the most direct approach to maintaining contact and stimulating interaction is to host contests.

We have already mentioned this sort of tactic where good content is concerned, but you cannot overlook it as a prime method for stirring up a bit of buzz. You can direct your audience to your website through social media, and you can then keep them up to date with the same channels.

Here's a good illustration:

1. *Your business can use Pinterest to demonstrate some concepts or lifestyles associated with your brand. You begin to develop a following and use Facebook to show some of your Pinterest activities.*

2. *You create a contest that asks people to first follow your boards and then to create a board of their own based on your business/lifestyle/corporate image.*

3. *They then leave a link to their board in the comment section of your Pinterest page for the contest.*

4. *You announce the winner via social media.*

This process keeps people watching and interested, plus you get to see and hear what your clients think about your business and how they view it.

The "Custom Community"

The last example is what is also known as a custom community. These communities are most commonly found as "hubs" for recognized brands.

From these central locations the visitors will engage in everything from games and quizzes to polls and commentary. They are usually brought to these communities via advertising, but they can also be sent to them via social media links.

The great part here is that the visitors will participate and be encouraged to pass along anything that they find. Often this is a form of WOM because the visitor will send along something a friend will enjoy or find interesting.

For instance, many contests have links or options for sharing via email or social media.

Custom communities also exist in the form of dedicated channels, such as a YouTube channel. The way to use these to generate interest is to make them interactive rather than strictly for viewing.

You can use the following ideas:

- *Use a brand wrapper that turns the social media page into a full blown branding experience. You can add video, music, links, a brand saturated wallpaper or background, and more. The point is to get the viewer fully "brand engaged" and then give them all of the tools for interaction.*

- *Ask viewers to submit videos or photos of themselves relating to the product or service.*
- *Provide helpful tools for submissions.*
- *Give prizes.*
- *Promote through other social media.*
- *Generally encourage the audience to have fun while working in the context of the "brand" or community.*

Next Steps

All of these ideas, however, may still leave you unable to get your audience completely motivated. A lot of good reasons exist for this to be happening, including the absence of a simple "call to action."

The next chapter focuses entirely on transitioning your followers, likers, and subscribers into full-fledged buyers. The part that is surprising is that it is often an easy process to accomplish.

Chapter Five

Motivate Audiences

Motivation is defined in a few ways, including the following:

The reason or reasons one has for acting or behaving in a particular way.

The general desire or willingness of someone to do something.

Provided with a motive or given incentive for action.

For our discussion, however, we have to condense these definitions into a single action:

Giving someone something to make them interact with your social media, which is designed to create brand advocacy and a sale.

After all, you have already directed a great deal of energy toward gaining their attention and retaining it. Now, the natural "next step" is for an interested audience member to invest in the relationship further, to make a purchase.

Because we are no longer using the classic "Buy Now" sales model, we have to begin to apply what we know about social media to encourage a viewer to become that desired buyer.

The question is "how?"

Understanding Conversion in the World of Social Media

Current statistics show that social media can provide up to 62% of a company's sales leads.

Obviously, this statistic means that it is *the* way to go where developing a profitable audience is concerned, but you really have to know what you are doing to transition those large numbers of leads into actual sales.

We will tell you that it is actually pretty straightforward.

Just consider the following:

You have already dedicated yourself to finding the right language and message to convey and are creating many social media and blog materials to do so.

You have made sure to establish ongoing relationships rather than going for the immediate sale.

You are also maximizing content discovery by creating multi-level forms of communication that prolong the "shelf lives" of your materials.

The above means that you are already well on your way to making social media conversions, but you still may need to do a bit more "listening," as well as ensuring that you have a very clear delivery of a "call to action."

Listening to Customers

Do you remember when we were discussing our total demographic analysis and the ways of finding out where your clients or audience might already be "hanging out" on the Internet? We suggested that you use some "listening tools" such as Google Alerts or Twitter search to discover what is being said about your industry.

That was a preliminary method of listening, but you also want to use listening tools and techniques to discover what your clients need to hear in order to convert.

For instance, you can monitor how people are sharing your Facebook content, retweeting your tweets, and more. Do this monitoring, as it is vitally important to hear what potential clients want versus what they are not interested in hearing or reading.

Just consider the following scenario:

Your Product XYZ is a gadget for the kitchen. You write one blog post about summer recipes and don't even mention the product in the tags, title, description, etc. The product is used in each of the recipes, but you don't make that clear until someone reads it. Later that week you make a blog post about the uses of the product but don't use the name for it. For instance, it is a chopper and you call the blog something like "The Use of Food Choppers." You see that a lot of attention and traffic was generated by the recipes, but that you got zero hits from the second blog. You know to note that the second effort was a flop and to avoid such subjects or approaches in the future.

You have to always keep in mind that social media is a dialogue, an exchange. When people repost, share, or otherwise take your message and spread it around, it is like a flashing alert for you to sit up and take notice.

With each share or retweet, your expertise and credibility are being established. When you nurture this by also being a responder rather than a broadcaster, you only enhance your chances for more and more conversions.

Here is what we mean:

You have decided on a fixed "content calendar" that has you writing materials on a regular basis. Let's say that you share information across your social media pages twice each week.

You get all kinds of thumbs ups, tweets, and shares out of this, but what are you doing in return? Be sure that you are thanking or responding to those who engage directly with the content.

You already know this, right? The reason we are repeating it here is because most of the folks who will post items will also leave comments behind. You need to "listen to" these comments and use them to uncover the next batch of materials to write about, the next line to develop, etc.

Reconsider the example we provided about Product XYZ and the two blogs. You may have seen a lot of comments in favor of certain recipes, certain uses of the device, and even negative comments about the ways that the product is not so great.

These are bits of data that you can use to prove to your audience that you are listening. You will create future blogs and materials that respond to such comments, and you will find a lot of positive benefits from doing so. You also have to consider the keywords you can take from all of your "listening."

Keywords—Again!

Just consider that many people beginning to do SEO and social media development will use different online tools to develop blog content. This tactic is sensible for a "startup," especially if you have not consulted with a professional.

Many websites now offer keyword tools that let you enter the term and get a list of possible short and long tail keywords that would be suitable blog topics for future entries.

For instance, you might have a site selling Judaica and want to blog about relevant holidays as they are about to occur. You go to an online keyword provider and enter the term "Passover." You will then get a list of likely blog titles or topics that will work well with your plans and intended audience's interests.

Of course, you will also be sure to integrate these blogs with your social media posts. The important idea to remember is that you won't have to use such resources for very long because your readers' responses are likely to really help you determine the best directions possible.

A Simple Illustration

Here is what we mean:

1. *You make a blog post about Product XYZ and its "green" properties.*

2. *To follow up with this post, you start a Pinterest board showing earth-friendly images and concepts relating to your product.*

3. *You also alert your social media viewers to the new blog and the short video you make about it.*

What does this accomplish? It creates a series of comments on Facebook that include a lot of questions and basic ideas. Almost all of these are fodder for further blogs and posts.

Don't ignore these interactions! Yes, you will respond to them accordingly, but you should also expand on them to show your viewers that you are listening closely.

Will that motivate them to make the purchase? It really depends. After all, they may just be waiting for a clear answer to a question before they go ahead and buy. They may also need that final "nudge" that is still referred to as the "call to action."

Luckily, you can often roll the call to action right into a response to a comment, question, tweet, etc.

Call to Action

Here's the key about the call to action: it is often considered to be a type of "ad" that is placed in the body of the website, but it is much more than that.

We have used them as any of the following:

- The button to push to "buy now"
- The area to click to receive a "free offer"(usually requiring an email or a "Like," etc.)
- A way of subscribing to a blog or newsletter
- A button to "learn more," which usually takes them to a landing page, website page, or social media page

You can see that they can be passive as well as assertive and are wonderful ways to just tell the viewer what they need to do.

Believe it or not, consumers are cued to seek out these instructional features, and if your page is missing a clear call to action it may seem confusing to most visitors.

This issue, of course, doesn't occur when social media is used because the "clickable" links and embedded URLs are the call to action.

How? Just stop to think about it for a moment: if a call to action is meant to inform or to provide a deeper source of knowledge about an issue, isn't that video blog link on your Facebook page a very direct call to action?

So give your viewers the solution to their problem by providing them with easy-to-use and very clear cut calls to action.

Tips for Creating an Effective Call to Action

Don't get us wrong, you cannot use some vague title for a blog, use it as the clickable call to action, and consider it a done deal. No, you have to create a call to action that does not feel forced, risky, potentially fruitless, or contrary to the established patterns of the viewer.

Some surefire ways of composing calls to action that will indeed be acted upon exist. Here are our suggestions:

Answer the inevitable "why?"

Why should that viewer click the call to action? Be clear about the immediate benefits they receive by answering the call.

- *Will they get constant updates about an issue?*
- *Will they hear news about new product lines?*
- *Give them a clear and positive answer as to why they should act.*

Give them something for it

You know this one already, but it bears repeating. If you are harvesting names through a call to action, give them something to "sweeten" the deal.

- A whitepaper
- An infographic
- A free downloadable report

Rely on active language

A call to "action" requires language that describes the action. Good examples are

- "Like,"
- "Register,"
- "Buy," and
- "Donate."

You can also create urgency. "Offer Expires," "Act Now," etc.

Don't hide it

Use contrasting colors, white space around the area, or larger/bolder text. Also, don't be afraid to ask them to act. If you have been doing the relationship "work" it is high time to encourage your viewers to make the next move.

Choosing the Right Language

What are some reasonable social media calls to action? That is a good question, and here is our list of active and preferred calls:

- Add RSS feed
- Add to favorites
- Add to shopping cart
- Add to wish list
- Bookmark this site or page
- Buy now
- Call now
- Chat now
- Contact us
- Digg this
- Download whitepaper
- Email a friend
- Follow on Twitter
- Forward to a friend
- Like us on Facebook
- Please retweet
- Print page
- Purchase now
- Read more articles
- Register for email
- Register now
- Request a catalog
- Review our product
- Share
- Sign up now
- Tweet this
- Vote
- Watch or play video

See? No pushy sales language and nothing that takes you way outside of the established relationship. Instead, you are encouraging people to take advantage of your established credibility and authority to interact in a deeper way.

Offline and Real World

Of course, a time will come when you may need to interact with clients "offline." Whether it is in a phone conversation, Skype session, private email, or face-to-face meeting you need to remain open and flexible. You have taken it online as far as possible, and if the client needs direct input from you, you must be sure that you can recognize the signs.

Naturally, if your business does not need direct "real world" contact, don't feel the need to take it to that level.

The point is to remain attentive to what clients and customers are saying. This conversation guides you in terms of the business and marketing and also helps you to understand if you are sending out the right message and doing so in an effective manner.

This interaction is all part of the listening and engaging necessary for good social media, but it also figures into the "measuring" aspect of social media sales.

Yet another essential part of the process includes the use of metrics that will assess social media efforts and determine if you need to change your tactics.

Measurement also indicates if your social media efforts are returning more than they actually cost to implement. This measurement is known as ROI (return on investment) and is the topic of the next chapter.

Chapter Six

The ROI Debate

Let's do a quick review because we are going to look at the ROI, the return on the investments, you are making in social media.

In other words, what are you getting out of the time, money, and thought you are directing toward social media?

To get an accurate answer we need to dedicate a few moments to review all of the activities into which you will be channeling your resources and eventually measuring or tracking for results.

The above is the essence of ROI, but let's just reiterate that your "investment" can mean

- Time,
- Money,
- Thought,
- Energy, and
- More.

Only you can fundamentally understand what is of value to you and what matters or does not in terms of "getting something back."

So does it matter to you if you get some sort of return from your time spent writing content?

Does the energy spent doing some networking matter as well?

Know the answers to such questions because they do matter. If you don't worry about spending two or three hours twice a week in composing your blog, then you don't have to "count" it as part of the investment, but that is not how professionals would handle it.

They track every moment dedicated to social media and use those moments to calculate the total ROI. They also consider "non-financial" returns as well, but we'll take a look at that in a later chapter.

A lot of experts insist that people are spending way too many working hours, and hours of free time, doing social media work. Whether they are monitoring, responding, or scrolling through pages of comments, it is imperative (they insist) that a clock is being used and time is being tracked.

Some marketers and sales experts say that an hour or two each day is the maximum amount, but others argue that 30 minutes is the total amount that should be directed towards this activity each day.

Essentially, they all agree that social media shouldn't take up a huge part of your day, but it can easily do so if you are not watchful.

When you look at the list of the social media activities you may have to tackle, it is easy to see why so many professionals turn to support from social media marketing firms such as my own, Sneeze It.

The Ever-Growing List of "To Do" Items

Just consider the items to which you will have to be attentive and give time:

- Ensuring you are responsive to all social media communication
- Learning the new sales model
- Understanding which social media are the most appropriate for your business goals
- Developing a "template" of the ideal client(s)
- Discovering the demographics about your ideal client(s)
- Developing a content strategy around all of the data including:
    - The type of business you do
    - Where you audience "hangs out" in social networks
    - What they are saying
    - The language they use to discuss and find your product or service
    - The strongest keywords
- Creating a targeted message
- Creating materials to "give away"
- Being ready to "learn" from your experiences
- Friending, following, liking, etc. others in your field and your possible audience
- Incorporating your existing contact lists into social media
- Attracting social media audiences by
    - Branding your pages
    - Establishing trust and credibility
    - Creating a blog
    - Enhancing the blog to ensure interaction and traffic
- Understanding how SEO will benefit you
- Generating top of the line content, such as
    - SEO blogs and traditional blog content
    - SEO articles and regular articles posted to social media platforms and article directories

  - Wall posts on Facebook
  - Interactions on Facebook
  - Tweets
  - Twitter interactions
  - Google+ posts
  - Google+ interactions
  - Profiles on sites such as LinkedIn
  - Pinterest Boards
  - Photos (including those on Flickr)
  - YouTube videos
  - Tags, titles, and identifying labels on all content listed above
- Creating a content calendar
- Focusing on lead generation through
  - Creating SEO content
  - Blogging
  - Finding common interest groups on all social media sites
  - Generating content relevant to your lead generation efforts
  - Advertising
- Focusing on retention through
  - Posting new content often
  - Enabling the sharing of content
  - Creating social thank you pages
  - Prolonging the shelf life of social media links
  - Keeping in touch
  - Networking
  - Avoiding hard sales
  - Creating an "expert" reputation
  - Giving away valuable materials
  - Interacting to the fullest extent
  - Developing a good "voice" in your messages and communication
  - Positioning yourself in the best "view" to your audience

- Creating buzz opportunities on all social media and website pages including
    - Sending them offsite
    - Offering games and contents
    - Expanding on blogs via videos, eBooks, etc.
- Focusing on conversion by
    - Listening and being responsive
    - Returning any social media favors
    - Triple checking keywords and blog subjects per audience interest
    - Creating a potent call to action

Yes, you are going to need to do all of that!

Usually, a glimpse of this list is going to send a lot of people running to places like my firm because they know that they won't be able to handle this mountain of material and ongoing work. That is always a good option if you know you don't have the time to commit to selling via social media or if you just need a hand with some of the tasks.

Remember I am partial to hiring consultants to guide you, support your efforts, and make it easier to determine ROI, but you can and should be trying this yourself at some point. It is a real eye-opener to see the interaction your brand has with its audience.

How? Always keep in mind that your social media begins as a learning process and then transitions into a sort of system. Once you have identified your key sources for leads or an audience, you are going to "refine" your methods. This refining includes subjects we will cover shortly such as building a tribe and finding evangelists.

The important point to consider here is that a great deal of the measuring does come to an end after only a short while.

Why? You will be doing activities such as choosing keywords and assessing their effectiveness, identifying your best type of client, and related tasks.

These tasks will have a return on financial investment that you can measure but will also have a return on the investment of time and energy you expended. You need to keep track of these items because they have value over the long and short term.

This is why we suggested that you create a content calendar and we also recommend that you track the amount of time you spend creating and distributing the content.

Let's just begin with a very basic discussion on the simplest ways that modern businesses measure their social media success. After that, we'll get more detail specific and scrutinize a few of the points we haven't yet given a huge amount of attention.

Understanding Measurement in the World of Social Media

How do you make the best decisions? Most of us will answer that we use available facts, data, information, etc.

Few of us "guess" when the decision is important.

The use of data is a good approach to decision making in general and especially in any decision making around a business.

We don't just do the research, however, and then hope for the best.

No, we

1. Do the research,

2. Gather the data,

3. Do some testing or theorizing, and

4. Then settle on a proven approach or method.

Thus, choosing to measure the results of social media activity is fiscally responsible and a wonderful part of the "learning experience" that you commit to when deciding to sell through the new sales model.

The need for accountability on each line item expense is imperative, and where social media efforts and rewards are concerned you need to use a lot of tracking to be sure it is "paying off."

After all, your time is equal to money just as much as actual cash, and you need to know that your investment has adequate rewards.

Measuring Tools

You will accomplish this "accounting" through the use of

- Tracking software
- Social media monitoring software to know who is talking about your content
- Analytical tools available online
- Attention to local rather than web-wide activity
- Tracking responses to targeted calls to action
- Tracking of failures

Understanding the Tools Available

Let's consider these methods.

The first three are all very similar. For example, you can easily find the following tracking software:

- **Google Analytics.** This tool looks at your website and tells you about every bit of traffic it receives.

Did someone come from Twitter?

How many hits on your landing page occurred from a Facebook status update and link?

Basically, Google Analytics shows you each step a consumer took before converting or making a purchase. Just consider the value of a simple report that shows you the "Top Traffic Sources" by the source, the number of visits, and the total percentage of visits attributed to the source.

This software tells you which blogs brought traffic and points you toward the most lucrative or rewarding subject matter.

- **Facebook analytics.** The Facebook Insights page shows you all of the activity around your Facebook page.

How many "Likes" have you received?

How many interactions?

Everything you need to know can be displayed in easy-to-read tables.

- **YouTube analytics.** You can use this analytics page to show you the "breakdown" of your entire audience. This page includes a huge amount of demographic information such as
    - Location,
    - Gender, and
    - Age.

It lets you know which of your videos is attracting the most attention, traffic, and visitation.

- **Twitter analytics.** Not many "freebies" are available in terms of Twitter analytics, but we can tell you that Twitonomy is a platform that is a free service (at the time this book went to press) and gives you a lot of analytical data about your Twitter account activity.

The remaining tools are not as similar as analytical tools:

- **Ignore calls to monitor trending.** If you have a small specialty business in a rural area or smaller city it is unlikely that you will be able to find any data on the big social networks about your business.

Instead, you will want to put an emphasis on engagement with your audience and on any local influence you have. Google Place Pages and video messages are great for this. So too is the use of long tail keywords for any SEO work or blogging and content creation that you do.

- **Calls to action.** When and how are calls to action successful? Ultimately, they have to be designed to indicate how they have worked. So be sure that you have them on all of your social media pages, and be sure that they head to a place that is easily tracked.

Though a website home page is a common choice, it is probably better to consider landing pages, too. We have mentioned them often in this book, but have not yet formally defined them.

In brief, landing pages are "subpages" to a home page. They carry an equally valuable message but often feature a sales- or lead-generating message with SEO text and the goal of capturing data or making a sale.

They are easily analyzed and will show you what lead-generation offers are really the most relevant and converting the best for your social media traffic.

- **Failing.** Remember that we said that social media work is about learning, and learning means you make mistakes or even fail? You can take a lot out of a shabby experience like failure, especially where social media sales are concerned.

Failure and testing go hand in hand, and you are going to do your fair share of testing; thus, you will fail too. Keep in mind that each failure shows you what people don't want to see or materials that are of no interest to your audience. This means you will refine, hone, and sharpen the message when you fail and use the lessons learned. Yes, it is annoying and "stinks," but it is to your benefit, too.

Using What You Have

All of the analytical data is a tremendous advantage. It shows you every single result from every single social media effort or blog post you have made.

Analytics tell you the following information:

- *Which links brought traffic*
- *Which posts created activity*
- *Which videos were viewed*
- *If people subscribed*
- *So much more*

You can see the analytics and tracking data, you can see when something really bombs, and you can focus where you need to because the data tells you so, but how do you actually use all of this?

So what if you got 400 likes on Facebook from a video you posted?

What does it mean for you and your social media sales goals?

What we suggest is that you keep these four questions in mind:

1. What is a qualitative goal for your testing and assessment?
2. What method will you use to get your data?
3. How will you know if you succeeded or failed at reaching that goal? Consider time, effort, expense, level of difficulty, etc.
4. What can you do to follow up on your findings? Will you stop doing something or will you invest more in the effort?

Goals

You can't test anything that you are doing without also having already established a goal or intention.

For instance, if we look at that long list of items you are going to be assessing, we see that one of them is "networking." Now, that is a pretty broad "goal" and is not going to be that measurable if left at that basic level.

Instead, we suggest that you say:

"I will get 200 new Twitter followers in the next 60 days."

This example is a very measurable goal and allows you to test the methodology that you use and to decide, quite easily, if it is a "win" or a "fail."

Something to keep in mind is that you might be tempted to do either one goal at a time or to try to implement a broad and sweeping range of goals at once instead.

The wisest approach is to make your list of content and goals and to partner up the most likely in order to "test" them. This partnering is economical in terms of time and energy and delivers data and results quickly.

For example, your goal is to get 50 leads from a video you posted on Facebook. A related goal is to get that video shared to people related to your industry. Your efforts might overlap a bit, but this helps to shorten the time spent on the work and ensures that tracking is made easier, too.

You can track these dual-purpose goals together or separately, but the point is to use as fast a pace as possible because "time is money" after all.

This is one of the main reasons that a strategy is essential and why the content calendar is a major tool of choice.

Methods

If you have followed our advice, you will have a content calendar. This calendar is a schedule by which you will post new blogs, comments, materials, etc. We cannot give you a template or recommended timeline to do these items because they have to be in accord with your business, product line, service, etc.

What we did tell you was to plan on creating regular, original content on a frequent basis and using it to create "buzz."

So if you are going to track your successes and failures, you may want to use the content calendar as a handy foundation.

Here is what we mean:

- *You have a goal of getting 200 new Twitter followers over the course of the next two months.*

- *You can make a worksheet or journal entry that lists the tactics and strategies that you used to do this. For instance, did you create a contest? Post teaser tweets about your video? Make a killer offer?*
- *Whatever it was, make concise notes about it and keep track of the precise text used. Then when those 60 days have come and gone, use your Google analytics and any Twitter analytics to measure the results.*
    - o *Did you get the new followers?*
    - o *Did they head to your website and convert into customers?*
    - o *Was that a goal?*
    - o *What were your time and financial costs?*
    - o *Was this harder than you anticipated?*

We strongly suggest that you use some sort of simple tracking software such as an Excel spreadsheet or a MS Word document to create worksheets or notes on each effort (there are many free worksheets online, but you will have to customize the data and headings).

This tracking allows you to understand the cumulative results of all of your efforts. Most analytic software gives you a choice for creating reports, and we recommend you use them and track the data.

Remember that we reviewed the analytics data in a list above, and that we also suggested that you track failures, calls to action, and anything else. Be sure that you use the identical methodology for gathering data to ensure that you are seeing the clearest picture possible.

Suggested Field Headings

To give you a bit of guidance in this area, we strongly recommend that your data fields include the following "headings":

- Date and time
- Page name

- Author
- Exact text of the item
- Google data about page: referring traffic, unique page views, time on page, total pages viewed
- Keywords used (keep headings for all keywords, including long and short tail)
- Goal
- URL that linked out of social media site: landing page, website, etc.
- How many Likes or Shares, all social media data (make separate headings for all of the social networks you are using)
- How many comments
- Copies of relevant comments
- Relevant page data (track numbers of fans, the URLs, etc.)
- Deadline
- Results: was goal met?
- Try to track "SOV" or Share of Voice: Divide the number of mentions for your brand/page/etc. by the total number of conversations in the market. You can use free online tools to get free data, or you can ask your social media marketing firm to keep track of this.

NOTE: Free "aggregators" can track the size of your community and your level of engagement. They can really help to determine the ROI for you while they pull all of the available data into one place. They are not necessarily the right answer, but they are great for giving a "snapshot."

We also suggest that you dedicate the time to measuring "sentiment." Whenever you find "mentions" you will want to manually determine if they are positive or negative. Keep track of this to see if your reputation is improving or declining.

Success?

Success does not mean you got a huge number of sales out of the campaign. It means that you met your goals.

Several hundred new followers is not necessarily financially gainful, but it might be!

This is why you have to have that initial social media strategy laid out: it gives you a clear "road map" to the goals you have to set and reach to succeed.

Just keep in mind that there are as many ways to measure success as there are to actually succeed. So ask yourself the following set of questions:

Did I reach the goal I set out to reach?

What did it cost me financially?

How much time did it honestly demand?

Was it very challenging in terms of effort and knowledge?

Do I sincerely believe it was a worthwhile "investment"?

Apply this set of questions to each goal and social media effort. This analysis is the only way to understand whether or not you achieved what you desired. That is really what you have to stick with, but it can get very confusing.

After all, you might say, "Hmmm, I got 125 new Twitter followers out of that. Doesn't it count for something?"

The most obvious answer is "Yes, it does." But you have to decide how much value to give to it. Did it take you four hours per day for two weeks? Then the answer cannot be "yes, those followers were worth the time and effort."

This is why the final step is the "follow up."

Follow Up

Where this step is concerned, you have two choices:

1. Do I stop this tactic because it is not working out?

2. Do I continue and try harder to get the results I need?

If something works out the way you had hoped, or almost gets there, go ahead and keep on trying to use it. It may be only a matter of tweaking the language, pushing a bit more on the "buzz" factor, or just giving it some time.

After all, isn't this the very reason behind testing and measuring, to find the strongest approaches and then "tweak" them with what you have learned?

If something has struggled along, however, and generated little to no interest it is clearly not a candidate for an ongoing effort.

This issue is vitally important, and we want to give it a bit of attention before moving on.

Making Your Choices

The return on investment, as we already know, can be seen as a financial gain but also as a gain in followers, leads, etc. So that can make it tough to know when to stop or continue with any of our social media efforts.

Of course, you have made assessments to uncover the most fundamental goals and are making measurements to determine if those goals are met.

Okay, you think to yourself, that's just great, but if my "goal" is taking up too much time to reach, does that count as success? Should I continue if it is really taxing my schedule?

Basically, you have to look at your choices from a "measuring" standpoint. You are going to make strong decisions if you are

- Measuring data,
- Making sure you have accurate data, and
- Coming to a clear and definitive choice after the measuring, testing, and assessment are done.

Whether you look at the end result and see that it was a huge failure, a moderate success, or a smashing success is irrelevant here. What matters is that you are now optimizing your time.

What does that mean? Look at it in the most optimistic manner possible. If you know what has failed you, you can take the lessons learned and stop doing it. This gives you valuable data *and* gives you back your time: you are no longer pouring time, energy, thought, and resources into a losing venture.

Testing is one sure way to know what you should stop doing, and this returns some surplus hours or minutes to your bank of daily time. Not too bad for a failure!

Knowing what to keep and what to cut is another way of saying that you are developing a list of priorities and discovering what areas to really direct attention and energy toward. This will reap the biggest benefits possible, but it also opens up an entirely new question.

The Broader Issue of Concern

What is this entirely new question?

What do we do about our findings in terms of social media?

Remember that this book is about *using social media for sales*.

So it means you have to have a sort of essential or foundational goal at all times, in addition to that basic goal for each campaign or social media effort.

That goal is to create traffic and leads through social media.

The goal is not necessarily making only that one sale per lead. We see how this impacts your social media work in two possible ways:

Will you work to get more traffic and to have more people discover the site and possibly convert?

or

Will you be working to keep the steady flow of traffic (traffic at the current level) but to implement strategies that ensure your conversion rate soars?

Essentially, you are always going to want to keep conversion in mind because it doesn't necessarily mean making the sale. Instead, it means that those who follow your links and make their way to your website do not leave as an anonymous person.

They will have accepted an offer for a bit of information, a newsletter, or a subscription to your social media page, etc. This essential dialogue is the core of social media for sales, and that is the focus of the work we have been considering here.

It is nice to know that social media traffic does have one of the highest visitor-to-lead conversion rates around, but we have already mentioned that it takes a lot of content to generate a lot of traffic and interest.

You have to dedicate the time to determine if you should try to bump up the actual conversion rates, or if those are good and you need to bump up the rate of traffic.

Clearly, those are two different issues, but it really all boils down to one point thanks to social media:

You have to establish dialogues that let you know your traffic's intent, and you then have to optimize to meet this intent.

How? Use the data!

The Cracks

Have you realized that analytical data can show you where and when visitors or traffic "fell through the cracks"? You have the data and can see every step that traffic followed to hit your landing page or sales page.

Did they all drop off at the landing page itself?

Is there a flawed step along the way?

Often what you will see is that not all social media channels are working the same. You might find that Twitter is not really the right platform for your clients, and that Facebook or Pinterest has driven a ton of convertible traffic to your site.

This information then requires further analysis because you need to see if that traffic did convert or if it dropped off after using a link or call to action.

Here is a moment, however, when it gets a bit tricky.

This is because there are no "average" figures about conversion rates through social media efforts. Yes, if you go online and start "Googling" for some figures, you will find a lot of references to 2-3% conversion rates.

That is just nonsense because it would not be worth anyone's time to put in so much effort to get such a slim conversion (100 followers on Twitter generating only two to three visits to a website? No, it is not worth the effort. Instead, you need to work with an expert to find the "benchmark" for your industry.

Social media marketing experts, like those at my firm Sneeze It, already understand how to gauge your level of activity against your industry in general.

For instance, they might tell you that you have four landing pages, but the average for your industry is eight. They will also have a good idea about the number of visits converted to leads that you should get to your site.

This type of market research is invaluable because the key to success is using social media but doing so in a way that exceeds expectations and leaves the competition behind in the dust.

You can also just start looking for business metrics about your area of expertise to find reports and other related data. The point is that no established "averages" exist where social media conversions are concerned.

Re-Emphasizing the Goals

This puts an emphasis on your need to set your established goals and seek to meet them. It is only *your* goals that can meet *your* business's needs, and that is what actually "matters," not your industry "standards."

For example, below is a table of data about conversion rates for a list of top retailers. Note how these vary from industry to industry:

Retailer	Conversion rate (%)
Proflowers (flowers)	14.1
Coldwater Creek (garments)	13.3
FTD.com (flowers)	13
QVC (online and TV sales)	12.8
Office Depot (office supplies)	12.4
eBay	11.5
Lands' End (garments)	11.5
Tickets.com	11.2
1-800-Flowers.com (flowers)	10
Amazon.com	9.6

How do they get these rates?

They test, fail, learn from the results, and begin again.

In fact, these groups tend to use very different ideas to create an optimized hybrid.

For instance, they don't test simple aspects such as different colored buttons or different images; they will use

- Different content,
- Different social media tactics, and
- Varied landing pages.

When they finish their testing, they have all of the data they need to show what "average" traffic is looking for (this is because they have usually tested at least two radically different ideas and pulled all of the preferred "stuff" from them), which gives them the model to use to continue to generate traffic or increase it. It might also be their way of learning how to optimize conversions.

So ask yourself what your fundamental goal might be:

Will you increase traffic to get more conversions or will you maintain traffic and seek ways of boosting the number of conversions instead?

Know the answer to that and you can get off to a very strong start. The next step would be to develop that list of goals and then get very specific about timelines, etc.

Getting it Done

Something we do need to emphasize and re-emphasize is the following:

If your competitors are doing "it" (whether "it" is a vlog, photos, or PPC ads) you have to do it, too. And you have to seek to do it better than they do.

Most often this is through the quality of the information and the option of something "extra." Added value is always the "hook" that seems to up the proverbial ante, but it has to be something truly valuable.

Yes, we have mentioned the use of

- Whitepapers,
- EBooks,
- Infographics, and
- Contests.

But we have not yet hit on hooks such as

- Coupons,
- Interactive materials,
- Rewards,
- Discount codes, and
- Games.

These are ideal ways of grabbing and holding attention as well, but we suggest some pretty advanced options that give your social media pages a very modern, knowledgeable, and instantly authoritative "look."

Always keep in mind that establishing yourself as an expert or authority is one of the simplest ways to develop positive word of mouth and consumer trust.

Methods for Establishing Authority and Credibility

The following tactics are great for building this sort of reputation.

Video and Podcast

YouTube is one of the major social media sites suggested for your use. The key is to do more than just make random commercials or mini-movies; the key is to create videos that have actual value to your viewers.

Yes, websites such as Animoto can allow you to make and upload a 30-second commercial spot for free, and you may want to do that for profiles and other similar places, but your videos need to be much more.

Let's start with some definitions to be sure you understand what we are talking about here.

Host. Both videos and podcasts need hosts, just like blogs. These hosts are firms or services that keep the files on their servers and allow wide and easy access. YouTube, Vimeo, Viddler, and Libsyn are some of the most familiar for video and audio files.

Podcast. This is a digital file (it can be a video but is usually an audio file) that can be made available for downloading to any sort of mobile device or computer. It is often meant to be replayed at a later time, but they can be "live" as well. The best have a few "episodes," which can have subscribers who receive the link to each file when it becomes available.

Video blog. This is the famous "vlog" which is a blog made entirely of video entries. Some call it video podcasting or vlogging too.

So how do these tools help you in your social media efforts? Let's just consider how we have already mentioned using them:

1. *You create a blog post that uses keywords relevant to your product or service. The words are related to previous blogs that have generated good traffic, so you want to expand on this success.*

2. *You create a video about your Product XYZ and the industry it relates to and embed this in the blog.*

3. *You send out links through Facebook, Twitter, and other social media sites that the blog is available. A few days to a week later you send out new notices about your newest video.*

4. *You also keep the file on a "channel" at the host site. For instance, you create the Product XYZ Channel at YouTube and allow people to subscribe.*

5. *You make sure that the video (or the podcast) has two or more episodes. This allows you to contact your viewers at least twice about it.*

6. *You then create a whitepaper that is essentially the transcript of the file and make this available through the same social media channels.*

Can you see the buzz this generates?

People might share your links many times, "Like" them, and generally draw attention to something because it contains valuable information. This information is always something valued more than a coupon, contest, or even a freebie like an eBook because it is immediate and hassle free.

It is also, hopefully, informative and entertaining, offering details that none of the competition has.

Guest Blogs

All of your social media efforts will have introduced you to many people working in the same field as yourself. Though they may never become convertible traffic, they can become advocates, allies, and supporters of your enterprise.

These are the people with whom you may want to address the issue of guest blogging. A guest blog is an exchange: you create an interesting, informative, and media-rich blog for their site, and they do the same for you.

The purposes for guest blogging are manifold and include the use of keywords, the creation of links back to your website or social media pages, and an author box that can also include useful data and embedded links.

For instance, you may create a blog about the industry related to your Product XYZ. Let's say it has something to do with cooking. So your blog is about late summer recipes and recommends the use of specific kitchen tools.

This means you are going to create "anchor text" that is clickable and sends the viewer to your chosen site, URL, page, etc. It also lets you use a brand name as a keyword, which is not something you would normally do in your own blog. It also establishes you as an authority because you are being published by someone else.

Interestingly enough, guest blogging is so effective for SEO that many guest blog networks have been created to allow you to find blogs that are a good "fit" for your content or subject matter. Just be sure that you are using the blogs with the best ratings or rank to reach the most feasible audience.

Photo-Sharing Sites

How would photo-sharing sites such as Flickr, SmugMug, Instagram, Photobucket, and others be of value to your social media efforts? The point is to distinguish yourself and your brand from the crowd of competitors. The easiest way to do that is with visuals or pictures.

Pictures instantly engage the viewer (and remember that you really want this) while they also promote your products, business, goals, etc.

Remember that one of the fastest growing social media sites is Pinterest, which is nothing but images. Users create their themed boards and then add images they like or appreciate. Businesses can also use these boards to speak with their audience in an entirely new and visual manner.

Step by Step for Photo Sites

Here is what we suggest you consider when thinking of using photo sites as your leading edge over the competition:

Start with goals

Yes, we know you are tired of hearing about goals, but this is no different from any other social media work you will do. So what is the goal? Will you showcase a product, a company mission, build the brand? Whatever your goal is, you have to know it and also know how to track success or failure.

Create some sort of unique look or "hook"

Photographs can be thematic and relate to your business in an innovative way. For instance, Product XYZ involves recycled paper. Show images of this recycling initiative or creative use of recycled paper goods.

Choose an anchor

A lot of businesses use a specific visual such as a piece of furniture, a landmark, etc. to include in their images. This is a visual cue that is very close to a brand name or trademark.

Label accordingly

Did you know that you can insert SEO tags and keywords into the names of your images? This boosts search engine results but it also ensures that people can find your website easily by using galleries of search engine "images."

Share

Allow any images to be easily shared by implementing social media tools on the pages or sites in which they appear.

Use them for contests

Pinterest contests are huge, and you can easily engage your viewers by asking them to participate with specific images. "Choose a color" for a new lipstick, "Name the dog," etc. These grab attention and generate a lot of sneezing.

Use new galleries to promote

Did you create a new gallery at Flickr? Use your other social media connections to promote interest and remain in touch.

Include photo sharing in measuring

You are taking time and investing in your photo-sharing activities, so be sure to measure the outcome. If you have established goals then this is just a gentle reminder that you need to see if the images are creating energy and buzz or if they are being totally ignored.

Advertising (PPC)

Hold on, you might be thinking, advertising is outside of the boundaries. Yes, paid advertising is NOT social media, but there is a place where the famous PPC ads (Pay Per Click) overlap nicely with social media. This is in the activity known as Remarketing.

Remarketing is typically defined as

An advertising strategy that allows you to contact users who have visited your website before. You send out messages or ads to entice them to return.

It is used to encourage guests who didn't convert to come back to complete a purchase or other similar step. It is also a tactic used for product upselling, branding, and social engagement.

How does it work? You create some great "value added" material that is shared across your social network. This material generates a lot of shares, page views, and activity, but you don't get sales or conversions.

Yes, you got the views and an increase in traffic, but if your goal is for higher conversions, this is the perfect time for a PPC ad. The use of a PPC ad at this time is going to be more successful because of the trust you have recently established with the viewer through the excellent free information.

In fact, they may not even be familiar with you until the social media campaign, and then after that they will immediately recognize you as the provider of credible and high-quality information.

Basically, a PPC ad through social media lets you put out your resourceful, educational, or entertaining content without any hard sell embedded in it. There is no "tie in" that turns off the reader.

It is free and they enjoy the benefits, but their acceptance of this offer has allowed you to open a door to communication. And the remarketing through PPC ads is a way to gently remind them of your value and to send out a call to action that will trigger them to respond in kind.

Be aware, however, that this PPC has to be a very clear reminder of who you are and what you provided.

For example,

1. *You provided a link to a free eBook download at your site through a Facebook update.*

2. *They clicked on this and "Liked" your page to get the download.*

3. *Now your PPC ad can say something as simple as "You Read the Book—Are You Ready for the DVD?" and have the "Act Now" button as the call to action.*

This is not a pushy sales tactic and is directly connected to social media activities. The viewer invited you to contact them when they joined your social circle and accepted that free information, and it is fine to contact them regarding the material.

We left PPC until last in this chapter to transition into the next. Why? The next chapter focuses on building trust and credibility. This trust is often fragile and can easily be broken if you go "off script" in terms of your approaches to social media and the related marketing tactics.

For example, using PPC may seem like it is pushing the boundaries, and that is why you must establish very strong bonds of trust first.

We encourage you to review what you have discovered thus far and be sure that you understand the many steps you will be taking in your social media sales campaigns. You might drop the ball or slip up in so many places, which loses the audience's trust and diminishes your credibility.

This is why we are going to spend a lot of time on these essential issues in the next chapter.

Chapter Seven

Building Trust

Trust should be "rock solid" once it is established, but it has a somewhat tenuous nature. Nowhere will you ever see this with more clarity than in the business relationship.

Whether it is a B2B (business to business) or a B2C (business to consumer) relationship, many actions can test and fracture bonds of trust.

This means that your "construction phase," or the time during which you build trust is going to have to be extremely focused. This focus is the only way to ensure that the foundation of your trust relationship is as strong as possible. Creating this strong foundation provides a bit of "breathing room" for those times that you misstep or blunder a bit.

Naturally, this brings us to the issue of how to go about developing and building up trust, and for that we have to turn away from technology and look directly at psychology.

Classic Models versus Modern Methods

So how do you know if you can trust someone?

What is the paradigm that you use when beginning to get to know someone (or a business)?

For most of us it will begin when we "read" facial expressions, body language, and the tone of voice.

Is this person darting his eyes everywhere but your face?

Is she sweating heavily?

Does he seem to cross his arms over his body in a protective stance?

Is she too direct and too trustworthy?

The list can go on and on! We read one another in so many ways to gauge whether or not we should listen and trust. Whether you prefer to read someone by his body language, word choice, or even facial expressions does not matter because the world of social media makes everyone invisible.

The classic model for beginning to learn whether or not someone or some business is trustworthy is no longer possible for the most part.

Why is this so? How do you go about reading reactions, facial expressions, and tone of voice over the Internet? How do you gauge a response to a comment when you cannot see the recipient's eyes?

You don't, but you can actually use social media in a way that is similar to the original method for establishing trust. How? While you cannot often look directly into a person's face (though Skype and other live video chat are options), you do have all kinds of measurable opportunities.

For instance, we've been placing a lot of emphasis on responsiveness. Someone can head to a Facebook profile and see that you fail to respond to many comments or questions.

What does that tell them? It says you may not be trustworthy, you may not be listening, or even worse, you may not be in business!

This example is only one online place that can indicate whether or not you are reliable. All of your social media activity has to be dealt with in a way that paints the image you want to convey.

You already know that you have to have a clear idea of the messages you want to send and know why you are choosing the specific social media sites. So you have to understand how to use them in a way that ensures you are showing yourself to be reliable.

Using the Methods Available

Fortunately, as we have been learning, different levels of communication are possible on social media.

We have the following:

- The blog
- Video links
- Podcasts and audio files
- Images
- Web content
- Social media activity
- Games and contests

Interestingly enough, almost any of these methods of communication can help a consumer or potential client understand whether or not they can trust us.

What we have to remember is that we need our social media behaviors to operate in very similar ways to "real world" socialization and we have to establish trust via the social media language.

For example, someone makes a connection by adding us as a friend or linking to us in a network. The appropriate response is to accept their request and make that bond. This, however, is the most basic way of interacting, and after that we have to take further steps to show what we are or what we have to offer.

That begins with making a good impression.

A Good Impression

Over the course of the last few chapters we have given our complete attention to the ways that this favorable impression can be established and used to convert "traffic" into "customers."

Let's turn this around a bit and begin to "humanize" the theory to show us how to use the modern models for sales and communication in successful ways. After all, if you continually think of the millions of unseen audience members out on the Internet as "things" that are not actual people, you will fail to communicate properly and clearly.

That means you should let go of the terminology; they are no longer

"Traffic,"

"B2B customers,"

"Shares," etc.

They are people you are going to converse with, socialize with.

You are using social media to network—remember? So your first point of contact should be the same as saying: "Hello, nice to meet you."

How do you make a favorable impression with people you are just meeting? You get their attention and tell them you are glad to have it. Again, you are saying "Hello, nice to meet you."

We've spent many chapters discussing how to do this in the right way, and we ultimately came to the conclusion that the first key you need is a clear and targeted message.

With this message you are ensuring that you are not clouding your new acquaintance's view of you with too much information.

Why not? Keep this example in the context of meeting someone new in the real world and working to establish an immediate sense of trust. Would you just yammer away at them as you shake their hand?

"Hey! How are ya doing? I don't know you, but I have this great product that I love, so I want to spend some time telling you about it and not really listening or watching to see if you have an actual need or interest in this. Did you say something?"

No, you would never use this approach. Instead, you would give them respect and convey a clear message of your intentions.

You create this clear message by actually saying, "I am glad to have this chance to talk with you and to share some valuable information."

You then would qualify that by going on to say, "I know this information is valuable to you because you have expressed interest in it."

How would they have expressed interest? In the real world they might make a phone call, approach you at a stall at a convention, make an appointment, etc.

In the world of social media, however, they have "pre-qualified" themselves as a lead because they have accepted some sort of initial offer or contact. In other words,

- They clicked a Facebook link,
- Followed a Tweet,
- Submitted an email to get a download, etc.

At this point in time it is not likely that they have "converted" into a customer. Instead, they are just starting to socialize or network with you. They have "just met" you.

Remember that we were just talking about the ways that the "real world" dialogue might work, but with social media it would be more of an "acting out" of such statements.

Just as you do in the world of person-to-person business, you will

1. Get their attention,

2. Provide the initial message (working to show how you differ from competition),

3. Listen to their response, and

4. Always reply, even if that person says "No thanks."

After all, if we return to the real world dialogue, you may have just said, "I know this information is valuable to you because you have expressed interest in it." To this, the other person may respond with a "No thanks."

Now, the best action for you to take at such a moment is to smile politely and sincerely and respond with "Okay, thanks so much for your time, and here is a pamphlet about us if you are interested in the future."

How does this pan out in the world of social media? The person says "No thanks" and you have the option of responding with a courteous and friendly "Okay, but here is our information" in the form of video links, downloadable materials, audio files, and more.

Through this response, you also have the chance to retain their attention if you have gotten them to network with you.

For example, if you have gotten their attention via a shared Facebook link, and they used that link to read your blog, you can also use modern communication methods such as an embedded video or podcast option that allows them to discover more.

Even if they still are not interested in accepting any calls to action, you will continue to have options of ongoing dialogue with them because of all the social media options that you make available. This might mean that they see the Facebook Like button, the "Tweet" button, the LinkedIn Share button, the Google+ options, the Pinterest Pin button, and so on.

If you are very clever, you will make sure that these social media buttons have tracking features that show how many others have used them. This is a "sub-level" of trust because it is a form of word of mouth.

Here is what we mean:

If you read an article and discover that more than one hundred others have "Liked it" on Facebook or that a few dozen readers have tweeted it to Twitter, you will trust the information a great deal simply because you see that so many others have as well.

Psychology and Social Media

This is social psychology at work. Let's just review this again to be sure you really understand what we are saying here:

- When there is a total absence of traditional social "cues" such as body language, facial expression, and tone of the spoken word, we have a hard time establishing trust.
- Social media is made up of blogs, social networks, email, and other forms of communication that keep the classic "markers of trustworthiness" hidden from view.
- We have to use whatever forms of communication we have available to help build trust.
- Building trust begins when we use the "classic" social model of getting attention, conveying a message, listening, and responding.
- We must also leave any channels of communication open but without the application of pressure. To do this, we provide a call to action that the viewer can follow willingly, and we leave options for them to engage widely in social media.

Though we have emphasized that few valid "averages" are available where conversions are concerned, some consumer habits can be noted.

For the most part, these habits tend to reveal that most people respond favorably to any chance to "think about it," by foregoing the immediate use of the call to action and opt instead for social media contact that allows them to watch, listen, and observe before answering the call.

Now, this sounds a bit disheartening, but it shouldn't. You can use this time to establish very strong bonds of trust by being totally responsive to everyone who speaks with you through your social media efforts.

Being Responsive

Consider the findings of Professor Judith Olson. She is the Bren Professor of Information and Computer Sciences in the Informatics Department at UC Irvine. Her studies on trustworthiness and the Internet indicate that "when only text is available, participants judge trustworthiness based on how quickly others respond."

What does this mean to you? It is pretty clear:

Regardless of your desire to respond at length or to use more time to send some sort of message, the need to acknowledge the social media activity is imperative in creating trust with the person speaking and with your whole audience.

Thus, you see a post on your Facebook page. You should not put it aside until the weekend. You should answer it within the next 24 hours, even if it is a simple thanks with a message about a longer response a bit later.

We can also acknowledge that this is a point where that older model of communication begins to fade in terms of effectiveness and even in terms of its viability.

For example, if you are a bit rude, uninterested, distracted, or just not attentive during a "one-on-one" conversation in the real world, you usually do not risk "fallout" in the social circle. This lack of risk is because often only two people witnessed the event—you and the other person.

With social media, however, the eyes of the entire network are upon you. So that person who posted a good question about Product XYZ on your Facebook wall should be acknowledged immediately.

It is okay even if you respond with something as simple as "Bob, thanks for that question. It is a good one, and I want to answer it as fully as possible. I will post a complete response by the end of the day. Thanks!"

The point is to be responsive and show that you are helpful, listening, interested in what the other people are saying, and ready to communicate. How else can you show that you can be trusted?

Just consider the following situation:

A person who has re-tweeted many of your tweets continues to do so in total "silence" on your end. You don't acknowledge their activity on your behalf or seem to give it any value. Will they continue to retweet your messages? Not likely.

If, however, you respond to one or two of their efforts with a tweet that reads "Thanks to @potentialclient, you're the reason I love my job!" or a similar acknowledgement, you will get support indefinitely. You will also show that you are a trustworthy entity to communicate with.

Checklist for Establishing Trust

To summarize, here is the "to do" list when seeking to establish trust online:

Initial Contact/Greeting

- Facebook Friend Request
- Facebook Like
- Facebook Subscribe
- Twitter Follow
- Tweet/Retweet
- Google+ Request/Follow
- Sharing of posts
- Blog subscription
- Connection via LinkedIn
- Following on Pinterest
- Viewing images on Flicker
- Subscribing to YouTube

First Delivery of Message (Being Responsive)

- Accept Friend Request
- Follow in Return
- Acknowledge RSS, blog, or other subscription
- Simple Email
- Post links to videos, images, articles, blogs, etc.

Listen to Response

- Ensure that social media buttons and widgets are available
- Track and measure all responses (Likes, Shares, Comments, etc.)

Reply

- Reply to posts, messages, tweets or retweets, comments, feedback, etc.

- Provide materials via links, URLs, downloadable materials, etc.
- Give a call to action
- Never fail to issue an acknowledgement, even if simply "Thanks!"

The Volume!

We know you are probably saying something like "Hold on there, a chapter ago you said to restrict the number of hours spent doing social media stuff. Now I am supposed to just be ready to reply instantly to all messages received?"

That is not really what we mean.

We mean that you have to respond in a timely manner—no more than a single business day after the other person has made contact. You can streamline these responses by using the tools that social media sites provide to help you keep up with your communication.

For example, Facebook, Twitter, LinkedIn, Pinterest, and other sites will gladly send you email alerts about all of your messages. All you have to do is use the links to respond to each post that a potential client has made or simply use them to ensure you know comments have been made.

You could also give over the duties of responding to someone else. My social media marketing firm, Sneeze It, offers response services for clients because responses are such an imperative part of building client trust. If you are stretched too thin, using a firm to write your responses is a viable solution to implement.

Which of the social media postings do you answer "first"? That is a sort of "non-question" because the most fundamental answer is that you must simply answer them all.

That does not mean, however, that a list of most important forms of communication for building trust is not available.

The Secondary Hierarchy

While your responsiveness to all social media communication is a complete imperative, and you must always, at the very least, simply acknowledge messages, you should consider something else.

You should consider which forms of communication work best in terms of establishing trust with your potential clients.

Yes, Facebook responsiveness to actual messages is more important than alerting Facebook followers to a video on the blog, but does a form of communication that will establish trust in a more concrete way exist?

Remember that comment about Dr. Olson's studies? In the absence of traditional social indicators of trustworthiness, when communication is comprised entirely of text, it is responsiveness that matters most?

So what happens when social media communication is made up of more than just written words on a screen? Is there a shift in the effectiveness of a message, in terms of trustworthiness, if it includes sound or images?

Again, we'll turn to Dr. Olson to discover what she found:

"For establishing trust, video is better than audio (with no video), and audio is better than a chat window. The logic of this hierarchy seems intuitive: people communicate as much, if not more, with how an idea is conveyed, than with what is said. Shifty eyes and raised shoulders can reveal anxiety; intonation can convey passion. The more non-substantive information the medium can convey, the more data a listener has to decide how trustworthy the speaker is."

To summarize, we must look at the use of "extras" in our social media according to this hierarchal structure:

- Video
- Audio
- Social media with images
- Social media activity with "text only"

This hierarchy means that most modern social media users still want to first use visuals whenever possible, which means that you can establish a sense of believability, authenticity, and trust by using video.

It also tells us that you should find ways to appear in videos, as this is what people are hoping to see.

This tip is much more useful than you may initially realize. How is that? Do you remember that we suggested that you ignore calls to monitor trending and other items if you have a small business and are seeking to measure your social media results?

This suggestion is because you won't "trend" on Twitter if you are a tiny family-owned ice cream company in New England (not unless you get unusually lucky) or any other form of small business.

You will, however, begin to attract attention and get great SERPs (search engine results pages) when you create videos and use them broadly. The tagging and describing of YouTube videos often allows you to appear at the top of search engine results, even if your site is not winning the contest in terms of SEO.

This fact means your social media videos can be leveraged to bring you a lot more traffic than you might expect—all while giving you a huge amount of credibility and trust from your audience.

Does it mean that only small businesses can use this hierarchal model? Not at all! In fact, we focus on this issue to demonstrate that all social media is still "social."

The old rules of establishing trust, including visual cues from body language, facial expressions, and tone of voice are still available on the Internet thanks to video and audio technology.

Thus, all businesses can begin to "put their best face forward" by relying heavily on videos, then audio, and then imagery in addition to their high-quality written content.

It is impossible, however, to create a winning "formula" that says when to use videos, where to put them, and what to make them about. Your own list of business goals is going to establish the ultimate list of priorities in social media sales.

A Simple Example

What do we mean? Just consider the following comparison:

You are a local provider of solar energy equipment. You want to use social media to broaden your client base in the region. Your approach to social media is going to be different from the national vendor of green energy gear and devices.

While you are going to seek to target the local market, the national firm is working to garner much wider attention.

You can both rely on videos; only yours have to be created to speak directly to your local audience. For instance,

- *Your video can talk about solutions for people in your region;*
- *The video can be educational and discuss buildings in the region using solar options; or*

- *Your video channel can be about DIY or solar "how to."*

The company looking to develop a national following would want their videos to be interesting to a less regionally focused audience and might include everything from solar energy in urban areas to methods of getting solar energy credits, etc. The point is that you can establish yourself as a knowledgeable and credible expert in your market, and you should use videos as a primary means of creating this image.

Is that where the creation of trust comes to an end? No, a lot more is still to be said.

Allies in Business

The term "brand loyalty" is a bit outdated but is still something alive and well in the business world. You can create this sense of brand loyalty through your social media efforts as well. The only part about it is that it is going to be unique from the classic model.

In addition to having customers who refuse to use any brand other than your own, you will also have customers who are personally invested in your business. No, not with cash and stocks, but they will be invested in terms of "promoting your company whenever they are presented with a chance to do so."

Here is how it works:

- Social media opens the door that has usually been firmly closed between you and your clients—they actually interact with you "one to one." Unlike the traditional "brick and mortar" setting, the online business owner gets to speak directly to each "customer" who passes through his "door."
- Your social networking and blogging speak directly to your viewers, and you are frequently sharing information, asking

for their feedback (advice), and never mentioning any sort of sales jargon while doing so.

- This gives your clients a sense of personal involvement, which is a form of deep trust and brand loyalty.

Just consider the way you might feel about a local shop owner who speaks with you whenever he bumps into you, but who never pushes his business.

Now, think about the way you feel towards a business owner who is constantly mentioning his business to you each time you "meet." Which one do you actually trust in that sort of situation?

- By giving freely and ensuring you are helping to solve problems, you have won allies and not just clients.

Here is what we mean:

Say you own an online specialty hardware store that focuses on vintage and reproduction products. Rather than creating materials about your different lines of goods, you create blogs about restoring antique furnishings, hanging moldings, and creating "faux" looks on wood.

You are giving away related materials that solve client problems, but you are not shoving a sales message down their throats. They look at you as an authority on the various subjects and consider you as their only preferred vendor because of all the good information you give away.

- Because of this strong relationship, you can also begin to ask your clients to leave opinions and feedback. This feedback is that amazingly desirable "word of mouth" that is going to do more for sales than almost anything else.

Word of Mouth, Reviews, and Feedback

There are so many statistics about the influence of reviews on consumer behaviors that to paint a truly accurate picture is impossible. Suffice it to say that a huge majority of consumers admit that it was a positive review or online comment that actually made their decision.

They didn't use opinions of other customers as a factor; the opinions were the only factor!

So if you can develop an allied relationship and then ask for feedback in the form of honest reviews, that is another massive step toward trust.

How are reviews requested? The most common methods include the following:

- Building reviews into a sales cycle
- Encouraging reviews with rewards
- Asking for reviews from vendors
- Creating feedback forums for specific products
- Asking directly on social media sites
- Following up after a purchase

So good reviews are great, but what do you do about a very bad review? *You leave it in plain sight.* No matter what sort of comments you receive, you have to respond, and you have to do so in a way that shows you to be honest, open, and respectful.

Remember that even a bad comment was made by someone who took the time to go online and leave the post. This comment deserves a respectful acknowledgement and must also be validated.

Don't ever argue in a churlish or childish manner to negative feedback. Instead, take responsibility for the complaint and guarantee that you are going to look into this matter to the fullest extent and try to ensure that the unhappy person does get satisfaction. Keep in mind that this entire issue is in the public eye and protect your reputation by showing a professional response.

What to Know about Trust

The ideas to take away from this discussion of trust are that your work at establishing trust is going to succeed when you

- Are focused on informing and *not* selling anything,
- Show that you are ready to solve problems,
- Take full responsibility for the good and bad,
- Are there to help your customers in any way possible—even answering endless technical questions,
- Listen and respond to every comment, and
- Are in it for the long term and not just to make a sale.

Social media trustworthiness is a very "layered" enterprise. A lot of work is involved, and many firms (small and large) turn to support to ensure it is done right. Their biggest worry or challenge, however, is when trust is broken.

How do you handle broken trust? The most effective modern method can be summed up in a few words: the video apology.

Keep in mind that videos are great for getting attention and helping to win trust but are fantastic to have available when a crisis strikes or when you want to issue a strong and effective "thank you." This is something we consider as we move into our next section.

Protecting Your Reputation

Your reputation is literally a "make or break" issue. A bad reputation will quickly impact all facets of your business. And you may have to work ten times as hard to undo one bad choice as you did when you were making the unfavorable decision that led to trouble.

Of course, not everything is in your control. Consider the idiotic fast food employees who have been posting images and videos of themselves doing horrific acts to food and the enormous fallout over them. Even a giant like Domino's Pizza faced some huge PR challenges over a single video post.

These are not actions that should actually reflect badly on the brand because they are the actions of idiots behaving badly, but the Internet is there to let videos go viral and there you see the "dark side" of "sneezing."

So social media postings can harm your reputation without you actually doing anything "wrong."

You will also find that disgruntled customers or unscrupulous competitors can set out to harm your reputation through bad reviews, nasty comments, and improper use of social media and the Internet.

Here is how that works:

- Your reputation can be harmed when someone posts horrible comments or images to your Facebook wall (this is why you make a business page and leave your private life to an individual profile)
- Your reputation can take a hit if someone leaves fraudulent comments on a feedback forum
- You might find that someone is using the comments section of your blog to post spam comments and outbound links to his own site
- Someone might "park" on your Google Places Page and mislead traffic
- Irresponsible workers might make videos about their work activities and leave them open to the public

This list could go on at great length. Also, news about your business can cause a decline in your reputation.

Fortunately, social media can be a tremendous boon, even if it is directly linked to the issue that is causing a problem.

Just consider the corporate video apologies available.

Apologize "In Person"

Take a moment to consider how many corporate video apologies have appeared over the past few years. Even if you have taken the time to watch only one or two of them, take a moment to reflect on how those videos made you feel.

Did you feel

Empowered?

Reassured?

Satisfied?

That it was authentic?

That it was believable?

That it "made things right"?

Most of the time, when the apology is sincere, you will feel most of those feelings. Why? Whether you know it or not, an apology is a social ritual. It is not ever just an "oops! sorry!" situation, which is especially true of a corporate apology.

While it is just a "given" that businesses of all kinds will make the occasional mistake, it is more significant to the creation of trust and the protection of reputation that an honest apology be made to the public.

Author Beverly Engel explains this perfectly in her book, *The Power of the Apology*, when she says:

"Apology is not just a social nicety. It is [...] a way of showing respect and empathy for the wronged person. It is also a way of acknowledging an act that, if otherwise left unnoticed, might compromise the relationship."

Notice that final word? "Relationship," which is what social media is all about. You have been striving so hard to create a relationship with each member of your audience, and if you want to protect that relationship (and your reputation) you have to take responsibility in every way possible.

What "I'm Sorry" Really Says

Business apologies have two very clear aspects:

They indicate that you are making a strategic move to improve your image.

You believe that you must take responsibility for an issue.

Regardless of what you are attempting to accomplish with the apology, you can create a much stronger (positive) reaction when you do it with a video message because it

- Conveys a strong sense of responsibility,
- Expresses complete ownership of the issue,
- Allows you to say aloud what you are apologizing for,
- Helps to show emotion, and
- Allows you an uninterrupted forum for indicating how you will remedy the issue.

The video also allows the audience to read your face and body language. The video provides places for comments, too, which says quite a bit about your sincerity and commitment.

For instance, how many businesses will open themselves to negative comments and humiliation? Using the video apology really puts you "out there" and proves that you have sincerity and integrity.

Just do a quick comparison of the options. A business can make a blunder, suffer a crisis, have a product problem, and decide that it is a good idea to do some PR and issue an apology. Their options are as follows:

- An email to all registered clients
- A written letter offering an apology
- A social media blast that includes a message from a corporate leader via video

Which "feels" most authentic? Is it the formal written notices or the "face-to-face" message from an authority figure?

Obviously, the video message works in the same way as an "in person" apology. The viewer sees the face, hears the words, and reads the body language to gauge the trustworthiness of the message—and most of the time they like and appreciate what they see.

Consider the fallout from that Domino's Pizza video mentioned above. A survey company gauged the immediate fallout and found the following results after the video and the corporate video apology featuring the company president were released:

Participants were asked: "Which of the following actions are you likely to perform in the next three months?"

	Before Staff Video	After Seeing Staff Video	After Viewing Video Apology
Go to Domino's Pizza	29%	10%	20%
Order Domino's Pizza for delivery	46%	15%	24%
Visit the Domino's Pizza website	25%	14%	24%
Search for information about Domino's Pizza	14%	10%	20%
Watch commercials that are about Domino's Pizza	61%	27%	42%

Interestingly enough, subsequent data revealed that the apology alone was not enough to re-stabilize the company's reputation.

The company had to find ways to regain consumer trust and attention and go beyond the norm. Fortunately, Domino's Pizza was already social media savvy and knew the best methods to employ.

1. It created a website around a contest.

2. It used social media to alert fans of the contest.

3. It encouraged individual franchise owners to participate at the local level (with many hosting smaller versions of the same contest).

This method worked wonders and has since helped the company to regain trust on all levels. It is a great example, too, of the power of videos because it was one video of two horrible people doing something to kill time, yet it threatened the reputation of a national company!

How to Do the Video Apology

It is important to know how and when to use apology videos to protect your reputation, and we suggest the following "tips":

Do it fast

Don't wait around for a few days to issue an apology. If you get right into the mess and make a pre-emptive strike, you can reduce the consequences of the problem that has occurred.

Mean what you say or at least "look" like you do

If your apology is more about saving face than actual remorse, you are going to have to spend some time studying the technicalities of the apology. How are you supposed to phrase the apology? What level of professional detachment works best?

Be human

It is very tempting to type an apology and make a lovely video of the text. The sad music, the gentle colors, and the easiness of it all may seem like a good idea, but it is not. Use the visuals to show viewers your human emotions, and let them read your sincerity.

Use the face in charge

If your firm is taking responsibility and making the video, put the person "to blame" in front of the camera. The person in charge and the person at fault may be different, but for a public apology it is always the leader who has to say he or she is sorry. And never, as in never, *use an actor to issue an apology.*

Apologize instantly

Don't make a speech or wax poetic about the times that try men's souls. Just cut to the chase and say how sorry you are within the first ten words. Make it an actual "We are sorry" sort of apology.

Emphasize your empathy

You have to let viewers know that you understand and sympathize with what they have experienced or are going through. This empathy shows you were listening and that you are going to make it right or as right as possible.

No excuses please

The viewers don't really need to know the background causes or your thoughts on why something like this happened. You want to focus your attention (and theirs) on the sincerity of your apology and what you plan to do to make it right.

Show the remedy

What are you going to do to make amends? Will you do what Domino's Pizza did and indicate that the parties at fault are fired and facing criminal charges? Will you do some sort of community cleanup? No matter what the plans, try to have a visual to show what you are going to do.

Ask for permission

Your apology may not be to the entire world, it may be to a few wronged individuals. Whether you are apologizing to two, ten, or one million, be sure that you have gotten approval from anyone you will name in the apology.

Post it everywhere your clients go

You know where everyone is hanging out online, so be sure that the video is made available through all possible channels. Also remember that your video(s) will trigger reaction. Be prepared to be responsive to the reactions as well.

Use your keywords

Just like any other video, this one should be keyword optimized to enable the most people to find it right away. You want to describe who and what the apology is for in your summary and insert the terms most relevant to your goals.

Say Thank You Too!

Videos can also be used as a way of saying thank you, and these can bolster your reputation and level of trustworthiness while serving to provide clients with valuable material.

Here is how you might use this tactic:

You create your social media strategy.

Within the strategy are ways of nurturing ongoing relationships with clients. Your social media contains no "hard sell" or call to action materials.

Once someone uses a link to a landing page or website he is given the same social media tools. He will see all of the popular control buttons that can allow him to follow you on any of your social networks. He can also buy the product now.

If he makes the purchase, does he get any sort of special thank you? The most common are

> *Thank you landing pages,*
>
> *Thank you email notifications, and*
>
> *Thank you triggered surveys or review requests.*

The customer is then entered into your ongoing sales cycle that continues to communicate with him around his particular needs or interests.

Do you see where a big opportunity is missed? It is in the thank you process. More and more companies are now creating thank you videos that provide a client with a huge amount of valuable information.

A Nice Example

For example, someone joins your social networks and uses a link to eventually purchase Product XYZ. She hits the "Complete Purchase" button and a new screen appears. On it is a "What is Product XYZ?" video that shows her the benefits of the product she just purchased or the ways that customers use it.

You can make this thank you video as interesting, entertaining, and valuable as you can, and it is going to also be full of further calls to action. You can make it outrageously funny if you want her to share the video, you might make it incredibly informative if you hope that she posts it to her Facebook wall, or you can ensure that all of the sharing tools available appear alongside the video as well.

This thank you allows viewers to subscribe to a video channel, tweet the link to the video, and so much more.

Remember that your use of these videos is going to do more than issue a thank you. It will allow you to optimize the videos for SEO purposes and to build on your credibility and trustworthiness.

Thus, the millions of prospective clients using the Internet to find your particular product or service will run across the thank you videos when they use the keywords you have chosen. These videos allow them to get an initial impression of your firm and to then follow up with all of the social media tools as well.

Understanding the Full Picture

Keep in mind that reputation management is about several ideas:

- It enhances your presence online

- It counteracts any negativity assigned to your firm or your industry
- It responds to negative comments or feedback in a professional way
- It strives to give you the best image available
- It is a form of outreach

Clearly, your reputation management isn't always about apologizing or saying thanks. As we mentioned above, you might find that some negative information about your company is on the Internet.

Someone might have posted a bad review, left unpleasant comments on a social network, or even be in the act of committing some outright sabotage on your professional reputation.

The reputation of your industry should also be considered. For example, many companies offering financial counseling, debt relief, and other related services face a glut of negativity around their work.

You might also have a good reputation, but one that is just too small to do you a lot of good.

How on earth do you begin to address these types of problems? Many workable solutions actually exist.

For example, at Sneeze It we provide clients with negative keyword domination work that actually identifies the strongest negative phrases and turns them around to generate traffic. We have seen as much as 32% of a firm's traffic come from these negative keyword tactics.

We also provide articles, press releases, and social networking to establish positive back links that all play a role in a good reputation in general. So answers are available, but they take effort and assessment to work effectively.

Handling Threats to the Reputation

Let's just use that list from above to determine the most appropriate ways to respond to threats to the online reputation.

Your Presence Online

Pew Research indicated that more than half of adult Internet users have used a search engine to find out about themselves. The result is often that the individual changes privacy settings on Facebook and social profiles, but it is also something that shows how a business might be able to enhance its online presence.

For instance, if you go online and perform a search for yourself, you will see the images in which your company name has been tagged or appears, the videos in which the tags contain your name, any and all comments or sites where your firm is discussed, and so much more.

This search provides invaluable information because it gives you a starting point from which you can develop a list of goals.

Will you begin writing press releases and articles that give a very positive spin to your image?

Will you make sure they are SEO to appear ahead of older negative comments?

Will you create well-tagged videos that help you to appear at the top of SERPs in order to get more traffic, enhance your reputation, and establish trust?

How are you going to ensure that you appear as an industry expert, even if you are the victim of harsh comments or criticism?

The answers you choose must be based on what you discover with your search. You may have a pristine reputation without any negative comments, or you may have a long list of sites in which you are spoken about badly.

Any of these items can be overcome through your social media efforts and your ongoing posting of fresh, positive, and beneficial content.

Negativity Assigned To Your Firm or Your Industry

We already mentioned the use and benefits that come from negative keyword domination. This tactic might include terms such as "debt relief rip off" that are used to create chat threads that lead potential clients to you because they position you as a solution to the problem. This aspect can be a bit complex, but we have discovered that it can create a tremendous amount of new traffic.

Negative Comments or Feedback

Professionalism is the absolute key here. You should see every single negative comment or remark as an opportunity.

The bashing of your name, the customer complaints, and the general negativity is not a problem because you can easily turn this feedback around. Direct contact—offline—is often the best way to go, but you could also use the "high road" technique.

Here is what we mean:

A client posts a negative comment about a project that you handled. Rather than explain your side of the story in a public forum, directly address the comment with a desire to do right by your unhappy client. Indicate that you want to remedy the situation and you hope they'll work with you to find an answer. If you keep calm and use a respectful tone, the irate person on the other end is the one who will trash his/her own reputation.

Will it take up a lot of time? It might. The key here is that you won't just be on the defensive. You are going to behave in a pro-active manner and do all that you can to create a steady supply of positive information that offsets the weight of negative opinions or posts.

Create the Best Image

This one ties right into the previous item. If you are to create a positive image you should be constantly striving to build a good collection of positive reviews, comments, etc.

Do all that you can to encourage people to submit such materials (this might be a part of the "thank you" process, in the form of a contest, as a forum on your site, etc.) and then get permission to re-use them as much as possible.

This positive material can go on your website, in your newsletter, as a press release, in a new article or blog, in a video, and anywhere it can appear to serve as a countermeasure to negativity.

Also be sure that you don't overlook the good actions that you do that are NOT directly related to your business. This need is the reason to get into such social media as Pinterest, YouTube, or Flickr.

In these places you can create videos or galleries showing the good works that your firm has done or is committed to doing. Be sure that everything is tagged appropriately and that you share this information freely on social media too.

Outreach

The new consumer model has clients searching for you, instead of the reverse. This model can be very limiting, and the one sure way to overcome it is to use social media as a form of outreach. This outreach is why you work to get their attention and to retain it over the long term.

As we said earlier, however, it takes only a few bad comments to begin to undo your hard work and put your reputation at risk. Because customers are always online and seeking you, you should extend an extra-long hand of welcome through specific online activities that include:

- Press Releases
- Articles
- Blogs
- Whitepapers
- Videos
- Photo Galleries
- eBooks
- Games and Contests

Just remember that you never work the "hard sell" into any of these activities because you want them to be valuable to your audience rather than a direct appeal for a purchase.

As you create these activities, however, be sure that they are fitting directly into your goals.

Remember that list we were discussing a few chapters earlier? Your reputation management has to fit into this list as well. So as you fill interesting materials with useful keywords, keep in mind that each piece may be a potential client's first impression of you as a firm.

This idea makes it pretty clear that you have to be sure your content is always the best, cleanest, and most valuable possible. This need to create such content is one of the reasons why so many businesses rely on "ghost writers" and firms like my own Sneeze It. Such professional "copy" is going to give you the best results because it has been drafted by people "in the know."

Just consider that one press release, article, or blog has to

Be original and unique,

Be truly valuable to your readers,

Provide outreach,

Create opportunities for sharing,

Be linkable to improve SEO, and

Reflect your company, mission, goal, etc.

That is a lot for one bit of content, but it does demonstrate how powerful the act of "sneezing" has become.

Never underestimate the power of your online reputation. Also, never underestimate how effective social media is at impacting your reputation for better or for worse.

Possible Hazards in Social Media

You may think your Facebook page is going to become an instant place of "warm and fuzzy" comments from your many happy clients, but what if it is just the opposite? What are your plans if you get a rash of negative comments about a major or minor issue?

Here is what we mean:

You create a Facebook page for your small bakery and restaurant. You have a sign on your door that encourages people to Like your Facebook page. You begin using it to advertise special deals, and then disaster strikes. You get an email alert that says someone posted the following on your wall:

"Hey Mary: I was in the shop yesterday and not only was the sandwich I bought horrible, but the girl at the counter was super nasty and rude."

What happens now? You started using social media to make your business better, to create an online presence, to get more traffic into the store, and to create a lot of leads, and with one message it is all at risk.

Is it though? If "Mary" used our advice, she would comment immediately about the customer's experience in a way such as the following:

"Hi Bob: I am so sorry to read about your experience. Please give us another chance soon and enjoy a free lunch on me! I am going to explore your complaint and get back to you with what I uncover about it."

You MUST then take the whole matter offline. Message him that you would like to discuss the service issue, etc.

The result of this approach? Your readers see that you responded immediately, did not just delete the comment, and even made good on a lousy experience. Anyone in business knows that people often complain on the spur of the moment and are just hyper-emotional at the time. Usually they react very well when a calm and pleasant response is made.

Above all, use common sense. I once went to a chain pharmacy in the Northeast to pick up a prescription for my wife. I saw the pharmacist filling another prescription, and she dumped a few pills on the ground, picked them up and put them back into the bottle. I was so disgusted that I looked up the number and left a complaint.

A day later I got a call back from the area manager who said he knew the pharmacist and she would never do such a thing. Remember I saw this with my own eyes so basically the area manager was calling me a liar. He and I proceeded to get into a verbal argument (this was before social media). Guess what? I never went back to the store again and told as many of my friends about the story. If social media had existed at the time I would have posted it to my 45,000+ followers on Twitter. What would that have done?

Nowadays you do not know how socially connected a customer is and the good or bad he can do to your reputation.

Of course, there are times when someone is just testing limits or sabotaging you. Explore the issue as much as you can, but get ready to walk away from battles that are just a waste of time and energy.

A lot of "noisemakers" are out on the social networks, and you may find that your best defense here is to turn the other cheek and focus energy on outweighing their negativity.

Some Simple Strategies for Social Media Trouble-makers

Here are our remedies and tactics for times when social media can lead to reputation problems:

Copy and keep the comments

You are already "listening" to everything your audience is saying. If a negative comment appears, be sure to quickly copy it and document it. This documentation is needed because some folks make the complaints but remove them right away. You still want to follow up with any problems.

Don't delete

We already mentioned this rule, but it bears repeating. Leave the site open and don't even block someone until that person makes it clear if his intentions are real or just problematic.

Never hesitate

Yes, it is so unpleasant and embarrassing to see a complaint just sitting out there in the open, but don't hesitate to act. Remember that news travels quickly, and bad news travels the fastest of them all. Social media makes ideas "known" in hours, not days, so don't put your reputation at risk by delaying.

Be prepared

Why not take some time to draft some responses to the most likely complaints you might encounter? Just as you have a strategy and content calendar, you might also want a "worst case scenario" strategy for negative comments. These also help you to avoid "blowing your cool" and saying something you might regret.

Create a tone

Will you be very formal? Perhaps you would like to create a less unpleasant setting and be a bit playful? Only you can know what will work in your industry; just be sure that you are never dismissive.

Seek guidance

You may not have the most appropriate answers when complaints are made. Consult with others, including colleagues, peers, people in the same industry, and social media marketing experts.

Know when to walk

You have to decide to whom you are going to respond and for how long. Also know when you have to take it all offline. All dialogues have a time and a place, and someone who is really unhappy with your company may need a very direct approach.

Monitor impact

You can monitor your reputation through alerts and searches. This monitoring will let you know when any news about your company appears online, which can help you see if there is "fallout" over any particular issues.

In the end, we encourage you to see your social media reputation in the same manner you view personal reputation. Does everyone adore you personally? No, of course not, so don't expect everyone to adore your business or product.

You will encounter bad comments, and some may be pretty fair while others may be off the proverbial charts. Be prepared to turn as many of them into opportunities as possible. Your proactive behaviors will sometimes prevent the comments from occurring in the first place, but sometimes you have to walk away.

The most important point is that you know what you can and should do to ensure that the millions of Internet users around the world can get the most accurate view of your business or product. Make your reputation one of your priority goals, be proactive, and you are sure to succeed.

Chapter Eight

Building your Tribe

The idea of building a "tribe" might seem odd, but stop to think what a tribe actually is:

A social division in a traditional society consisting of families or communities linked by social, economic, religious, or blood ties, with a common culture and dialect, typically having a recognized leader.

A distinctive close-knit social or political group.

A group or class of people or things.

Okay, so that is pretty clear. Tribes are groups that share specific links, but one word is missing from those definitions, however, and that is "cohesive."

Tribes are certainly all of the aspects described above, but above all else they are going to be cohesive or unified. They will not be made up of identical people but instead will be full of people with a common view, goal, or desire.

For example:

The tribe that wears the same brand of shoes.

The tribe that uses the same "green" cleansers.

The tribe that eats at the same restaurant.

The tribe that participates in the same social organization.

Clearly, the list of possible tribes is endless—the tribe of Star Wars, the tribe of Juicy Fruit gum, and so on.

Now, as a business professional or someone searching for a group of people who are united behind a product, service, idea, etc., why wouldn't you want a tribe?

The Benefits of Tribes

Here's some great news:

All of your social media efforts are identical to "real world" tribe building.

You are going to use your comments, communication, and social media language to find people with the qualities you need.

Remember that "template" from the first chapter? Your tribal members will all fit right into it.

Of course, social media is a great tool for tribe building because it is already working to find a group of people, a network, which shares common interests, values, desires, and goals. One of the most unusual facets of social media is that it does something that rarely happens in the real world—it requires that most of your viewers accept you as you are.

Stop and consider what that means:

1. The new consumer model sees the buyer seeking the vendor not the reverse.

2. The consumer does this searching through a set of specific criteria (keywords and search engine terms).

3. Once the consumer locates a list of choices (SERPs), she then makes her decisions about which of the tribes to join (pages to view and register with) based on the conditions, traits, mission, etc. she finds there.

4. Thus, the buyer or audience member takes you at face value; in fact he seeks you out for that particular "face." You cannot find this face value in the real world, and it makes online tribe building much easier.

How so? Just consider for a moment: in the real world of business you might struggle to depict a company culture, a mission, or the value of a product in a visual way.

Face Value

How do you "show" visitors how you want to be viewed or seen? You have to consider the creation of an image that includes physical and tangible decor as well as the products you will sell. You have to establish an entire physical atmosphere that is unnecessary in the online world.

The online world, however, is all about text, the messages, and the visuals that you provide at your social media pages or on your website. It is very controlled, which means your research and efforts will pay off because you will know how to speak most directly to your intended audience.

You also have the benefits of knowing how SEO works. That means you can learn the "lingo" or the language that your "tribe" speaks, and then use these terms in all of your text, videos, tags, etc. to be sure that they find you.

You will also be seeking them out using the same terms and looking for them on social media sites of all kinds. When you find groups, pages, businesses, professionals, and individuals who fit your "template" you will follow them and grab their attention. They will then investigate and join your tribe if you are a "good fit" for their needs.

It also means that if you are trying to build a tribe, you are seeking to create a group that will not necessarily buy from you but will always

- Follow you,
- Help spread the word about you,
- Nurture the strength of your business,
- Help you to constantly refine and clarify your "message," and
- Generally give you an enhanced social media presence.

You might think that is not really beneficial, but stop to consider large-scale companies that you already know that have a strong company culture but which may not see a lot of sales from their fans or tribe.

Tribal Culture

An endless list of companies with a whole culture built up around them that don't necessarily generate tremendous sales from all of their fans, advocates, or tribal members exists. These companies do, however, garner huge benefits from their loyal followers.

Just remember that list of tribal types we gave a bit earlier: the tribe that loves Star Wars, as an example. Do these folks buy only the films? No, they are into the culture.

Thus, you will find members of this particular tribe who get into the mythology, the music, the many types of paraphernalia, and so on. This tribe has many "niches" and they all overlap nicely.

This is precisely how and why you must work on building a tribe for your business and one that relates to your industry but is not always directly connected to it.

Think about this marketing concept:

A market tribe is essential for defining your business world. Members of your tribe share ideas and validate each other. Tribe members inspire each other to explore the extent of their thoughts and beliefs by social exchanges and debates.

Whenever such a group of people with common interests gets together, a synergy is developed. This synergy allows them to create something much greater than any of them could have created individually or in smaller groups.

Does this sound familiar? It should because we have been continually talking about the "learning process" that has to occur as you develop a social media campaign. When you put it into the context of building a tribe, you begin to see how and why social media works so well for sales.

Consider that your tribe (which is actually your converted visitors or ongoing audience) will

- Give you ideas;
- Provide feedback;
- Stimulate you to consider new ideas, products, etc.;
- Keep you honest by demanding constant responsiveness;
- Spread the word about your business;
- Participate in all of your activities (including real world activities, contests, etc.);
- Call you out when you are doing something wrong or badly; and
- Give support when it is needed.

Social media is a dialogue, and nowhere will this dialogue become more effective and even measurable than when it occurs between a group of "familiars" who freely share thoughts, ideas, and concepts in an informal exchange.

Just look at regular Facebook walls: friends post comments to one another, give the "thumbs up" to lots of posts, and generally show encouragement. These same actions could easily occur with a Facebook business page if you use a tribe building mindset within your work too.

Now, don't get this wrong—it is an advanced tactic, and it would be wisest to use it to expand on your *existing* groups rather than when you are just getting started.

Either way, here are our tips for building your online tribe.

Tribal Building Step by Step

Create a tribal member model

Before you start to even begin thinking in the "tribal" mode, also consider the ideal "template," or list of qualities you think a member of your tribe should have. Keep the idea of "overlap" in mind.

Let's stick with that Star Wars example and say that you sell Star Wars items that range from prop light sabers to costumes and books. You will want your tribal members to include those who are interested specifically in such goods, but you also want people who enjoy similar genre films, comic books, and many other closely related concepts.

Consider the keywords and search terms

You will seek out and find members of your tribe by using appropriate terms and then by beginning to follow or interact with those who are associated with them. They will do the same, and you can use a single idea or word to begin building your tribe.

For example, if Product XYZ is related to solar energy, you can use that single term on almost any social media network to find many new members for the tribe. You also use the "niche" keywords such as "solar chargers," "homesteading," and more.

Find "groups" in social media relating to your business

These are pre-existing tribes that you might get to join yours in one fell swoop. Participating in such groups is also a good approach to finding members to recruit.

Think of those you know

It is highly likely that you already know people who belong in your tribe; consider if they are good choices as "evangelists" (more on that word in a bit). If they can spread the word about your business to others who might be a good part of the tribe, be sure to open a dialogue with them.

Reverse the situation

Do you know two people who are not necessarily in your tribe but who would benefit from knowing one another? Make the introduction and connect these people. It is going to directly benefit you because their developing bonds will also include bonds with you, which is precisely how effective networking and tribal culture work.

For example, you know someone who sells "green" household goods like eco-friendly paint and sealants. Your site focuses on earth-friendly decor. You recruit a tribe member who sells cork and natural flooring. Introduce him to your earth-friendly paint and sealant friend as you all benefit from knowing one another.

Establish tribal patterns

Do you have a "thing" that you do across your social media on a regular basis with the tribe?

For example, do you have a day of the week when you encourage tribal members to post questions or stories on your page?

Maybe you have one day of the week when you need to point everyone toward a useful link you have found?

We know of a popular social media site that has a "Therapy Thursday" for its members.

Whatever will benefit the group will benefit you, so find ways of keeping the conversations flowing through regular exchanges, events, patterns, etc.

Cultivating Brand Evangelists

By now, we are running into a bit of a dilemma, and that is how to "distinguish" the members of your tribe.

For example, are they a potential buyer or are they an evangelist?

Maybe they are both? Perhaps they are neither?

These two types of members are quite different, so we turn our attention to the idea of brand evangelists.

Any business or professional who takes the time to listen to his audience will find a lot of opportunities for strength and growth.

We pointed out the value of failures and also have emphasized the need to look at all social media activity as a learning experience. We just introduced the idea of a tribe, which is a group that develops out of specific "commonalities" such as shared interests. Thus, tribal members may present you with ideal evangelists, too.

What is an evangelist? For our purposes, an evangelist is best seen as a zealous advocate.

Thus, the guy you know who cannot get enough Pringles potato chips or the lady who swears by her particular brand of wrinkle cream are true fans of their product, and because they tell you about the product with great enthusiasm they are also evangelists.

Though they reap no immediate benefit from encouraging others to use their favorite "this or that," they are more than happy to talk about it and "spread the word."

Can you see how beneficial it would be to find tribal members with that kind of enthusiasm about you?

Imagine what these folks can do on the social networks each time they post comments or share information about you.

What can they do? Let's take a moment to return to those comments a few chapters back about "word of mouth."

Evangelism and WOM

We have learned that social media can be viewed in the same context as word of mouth, or one person telling another about something. We also understand that the latest Nielsen data says that people trust advertising less than recommendations from friends or fellow consumers.

So, when people use social media to recommend something, that recommendation is often seen as far more realistic and believable than a PPC or other type of advertisement.

What does that mean in terms of evangelism? Your brand evangelists are going to be an ideal form of word of mouth because they are going to use their own social media connections to express their opinion, their positive and enthusiastic opinion, online.

The "kicker" here, however, is that they are telling people who are far more likely to have a similar interest in what they are advocating. Most people naturally tell "friends" about products that they know are of interest or importance to them.

Here is what we mean:

You have a small microbrewery in New England. You have a good Facebook following and share information such as press releases, new videos, and images of your products. Your fans can post or share the information you make available. Most of these people will be sure to share such items with their friends who would most likely buy your beer or seek out further information about it.

Those who receive the messages from your evangelists also have their tribes and peer groups. They show people this new "secret" and begin giving attention to the business.

You won't have evangelists broadcasting mindlessly without also taking in and exchanging information. Social media and brand evangelism are often called "conversational marketing." They use multiple channels of information that help your fans to share their enthusiasm and depict a very accurate image of your business or company.

Here is where we have to once again place a heavy emphasis on the content.

Content is Always King

Social media is not *you* talking about *you*—that is a recipe for disaster.

No one wants to read how wonderful you think your brand, mission, or ideas might be. They will, however, accept these accolades when received from evangelists who get no direct benefit from boasting of the wonderfulness of your brand.

Social media is you telling your audience interesting and relevant information that has no call to action or pressure to "buy now."

Remember that your content has to be

- Unique,
- SEO rich,
- Compelling,
- Related to your industry,
- Easy to share,
- Layered with blog, video, etc.,
- Ongoing and frequently updated,

- Engaging and something that triggers conversation, and
- Well planned.

Keep in mind that your tribe building and search for brand evangelists has to come after you have already started to establish yourself with a social media presence.

When to Seek an Evangelist

The "order of events" still looks like the following:

1. Creating a social media strategy
2. Creating targeted messages
3. Creating an ongoing supply of materials that are given away
4. Branding and enhancing social media pages that include (not in any particular order)
    a. SEO blogs and traditional blog content
    b. SEO articles and regular articles posted to social media platforms and article directories
    c. Wall posts on Facebook
    d. Interactions on Facebook
    e. Tweets
    f. Twitter interactions
    g. Google+ posts
    h. Google+ interactions

i. Profiles on sites such as LinkedIn

j. Pinterest Boards

k. Photos (including those on Flickr)

l. YouTube videos

m. Tags, titles, and identifying labels on all content listed above

5. Retaining the audience by

a. Posting new content often

b. Enabling the sharing of content

c. Creating social thank you pages

d. Prolonging the shelf life of social media links

e. Keeping in touch

f. Networking

g. Avoiding hard sales

h. Creating an "expert" reputation

i. Giving away valuable materials

j. Interacting to the fullest extent

k. Developing a good "voice" in your messages and communication

    l. Positioning yourself in the best “view” to your audience

6. Creating buzz opportunities on all social media and website pages, including

    a. Sending them offsite

    b. Offering games and contests

    c. Expanding on blogs via videos, eBooks, etc.

    d. Focusing on conversion by

        i. Listening and being responsive

        ii. Returning any social media favors

        iii. Triple checking keywords and blog subjects per audience interest

        iv. Creating a potent call to action

7. Refining your messages and establishing trust

8. Doing ongoing reputation management

9. Looking at the ways you can begin to really enhance your social media potency and to build a tribe around “niches” in your line or market

10. Growing evangelist relationships

We would suggest that you view the last two items as a combination of activities. Why? It is difficult to get someone to feel passionate about an entire brand but is much easier to get them talking about a particular item you sell or do, mentioning the brand all the while.

For example, a particular type of soda has big fans, but they may not be totally enamored with every product that company makes. When they mention that flavor of soda or that product, they do always mention the brand.

So you have to recognize those members of your tribe who will be reliable buyers and those who will really fall in love with your particular brand or product and tell others. You can then find ways to encourage them to speak out about your company.

Some "tried and true" ways of encouraging them exist, but it all begins when you organize your content to create these valuable situations.

Honing Your Tactics

As we already indicated, it is going to be a bit of a challenge to get to this point immediately. Instead, you have to have already developed a lot of your content and strategy before you can find the groups that will get talking, sharing, and sneezing.

Once you reach this point, we suggest the following tactics as the most successful methods of firming up your relationships with evangelists:

Bowing

Acknowledge any sort of milestone or give thanks to those who made it happen.

For example, you posted a new video blog on Facebook and kept track of the tribal members or evangelists who shared it. When it hits

100, 500, or more likes you then give those sharing followers a call out or tell them to "take a bow."

Check-ins

This is a wildly popular way to get your fans sharing and evangelizing. All you do is post the details about a promotional activity that is redeemable when that person can show or indicate the receipt of a message through social media.

Dunkin Donuts did this in Boston and targeted college students—the results were unbelievable.

Hallmarking

Anything that has an anniversary or notable date can be used to create evangelists.

For example, noting the number of times a person has shared materials is a good way of enhancing the evangelist relationship.

Huddling

Huddling is a chat or conversation with two or more, focused on a single subject. The most common place for this is Twitter though a Facebook page is a good option, too.

Must Reads

This is a call to action, but not to buy or to visit a landing page. Often it is best to send out a "must read" that relates to your industry.

For example, you are that seller of Star Wars related goods and you see an artist who has just made posters for the movies using her own particular style. Mentioning this artist as a "must read" will earn you respect and evangelists.

Mysteries

Random and mysterious, these posts generate activity and interest. Try to think of something that gets people talking and commenting, and be absolutely sure you can keep up with the responses.

For example, as that vendor of Star Wars collectibles and paraphernalia you make a random post about one of the Star Wars movies and ask others to give their feedback. Get ready for a lot of interaction, and be ready to find yourself getting a lot of new followers.

News Flashes

"This just in..." is a great way to grab attention, but it is also a way of creating a keyword heavy message.

It is an ideal way of posting video and visual content about your business, a new employee, a client's feedback, and more.

Photographs

This is *the* hottest way of attracting attention and using your evangelists who will happily share a good photograph relating to your business or mission.

For example, that Star Wars vendor might head to a convention and get a snapshot of movie stars making live appearances—talk about mileage and lots of new evangelists who show up looking for more similarly valuable content.

These tactics are some of the best in terms of conversing and providing your evangelists with ongoing supplies of material to share in order to show their love of your brand or product.

Troubleshooting Evangelism

If you are still having some trouble using evangelism for your benefit, we have some essentials that tend to tip the scales in your favor. Consider the following:

Pursue them and make yourself well known

Your possible evangelists may know of you, your brand, your social media pages, and more. They may not, however, know that they are going to be in love with you yet. To trigger their amorous feelings you have to speed up the rate of engagement.

Our preferred method is to put their *blogs into an RSS reader and try to respond to new comments as soon as possible. We also use email alerts for social media sites that alert us to any comments by our potential evangelists. We then continue our dialogue that way.*

Promote them a lot

The reciprocation factor is at work here, and it works like nothing else you've seen.

They share a link to something relating to your industry—share it.

They put up a post with a great picture—share it.

Be sure, however, that they know you are doing this. With Facebook it is easy for them to see, but with media such as Twitter you have to be sure tags are applied.

Soon, you will see that they return the favor and become a true evangelist of a brand or product that has done them a lot of good.

Step offline

Why not send a written message, an email, or a corporate gift that takes it to a personal level.

For example, if they asked for a guest blog, posted a review, or are just a powerful evangelist of all that you do, reward them with a free t-shirt, box of candy, or another sort of "real world" gift that acknowledges them personally.

Now, don't think that you can just go "all out" when seeking evangelists because they may not even provide you with any sort of benefits. Instead, you have to consider the entire issue of ROI where evangelism is concerned.

The ROI

Do you remember the various tools for measuring we mentioned in a previous chapter? We said that measuring was essential if we were to be sure that we got the appropriate ROI or return on the investment.

We came to see that our "investments" translated to dollars but also to time and energy. Now, a bit of a trap is here where ROI and evangelism are concerned because you have to be able to understand if any evangelist is going to generate the necessary amount of interest to offset the "costs" of acquiring them.

Consider that SROI (Social Return on Investment) translates to the "non-financial" returns sought by a social entrepreneur.

What does that mean?

An SROI Step by Step

You have your Product XYZ, and you create a good social media audience around it. Now is the time to consider how you can strengthen and enhance your image by the use of evangelism.

Take a look at existing fans, clients, and social media "friends."

See the data and learn that a very large number of these people frequently share your posts or your content.

Assess the content that they share and see the different "themes" that they are most interested in re-tweeting, sharing, or otherwise spreading to their social networks. (You will do this assessment all the time to measure when you should continue with any campaign and when you have to stop because it is a "dud.")

Begin to create goals around your tribe building and evangelist recruiting. This step is essential and begins with some targeted questions

What theme is most important to your overall goals?

For example, your broad social media goal is to build your traffic and to boost sales.

You are hoping to promote and sell a new product through this social media work but to a less likely pool of buyers.

Your newest content is generally about that specific item.

You have three or four themes for the content that you create, but only one theme is going to give you the type of "niche" traffic you desire.

Which of the evangelists seem the most interested in that theme?

By answering the questions from above, you can identify which of the evangelists are sharing, tweeting, or spreading the word about this theme. You can make this identification by analyzing the data and making note of those who have shared or drawn attention to specific content. You will be able to see where your sources of "traffic" are coming from, too, which also helps you create the right messages.

What sort of materials can you begin to create to get them sharing even more?

Clearly, you already know what they are sharing and where you need to guide the flow of future dialogues. Creating content around the theme that is already popular encourages more sharing, etc.

You create a new content calendar that includes an expanded list of keywords and topics, and you consider how to use them in blogs, video, and audio materials, as well as photos.

What measures do you have in place to see the effects of their evangelism?

You use the same analytics as you have in the past to see how often your new materials are shared and what sort of traffic these generate. For example, you monitor how many visitors appeared at the website from a single "share" on Facebook by one of your evangelists.

You need to give close attention to the number of new evangelists that appear and how often they begin to share items, too. You notice that one of the newly acquired evangelists is sharing stuff frequently—track these numbers as well.

Keep a watchful eye on your website analytics as this shows how many new visitors head to the website from the links and targeted content.

Can you see that we never mentioned any sort of financial returns here? That is because your initial concern is to see how much activity and "buzz" has been generated by the "sneezing" done by evangelists and their social groups.

Only you will know how many hours you have dedicated to this work and whether it is going to "pay off" in terms of your goals. The key issue here is to track the amount of time and the amount of interest and evangelism that your efforts have created.

While the typical goal of any evangelism and tribe-building work is to get more followers, remember that the underlying goal should also be that your brand becomes the one that automatically comes to mind whenever the product or service is mentioned.

Your evangelists will always hear words associated with your field and automatically name you as the ideal provider.

Try this game as an example of what we mean. Use it on others to get a strong and clear idea of the effectiveness of brand evangelism, a tribe, and a clear audience.

A Quick Game

Read the words in the following list, and then say out loud the name of a firm or brand that you already know:

Read the Word	Name a Brand
Chicken	
Pens	
Sneakers	
Lawn care	
Paint	
Pots and Pans	
Tax Preparation	

Wouldn't you want your business name to spring to people's lips when they read a word that describes it?

This is one of the goals of evangelism, and though it doesn't always generate measurable dollars right away, it can give you this sort of trusted status. Understand that this applies to the local as well as the national or global level.

It starts with your list of goals and the creation of buzz and a good image. It continues on as you build a tribe and evangelists that liken your brand to the top name in the field. Such a reputation is hard to value in terms of dollars and cents but is one of the many beneficial results of your social media efforts.

It would be tremendously beneficial right now to take a few steps away from this emphasis on targeted brand advocacy and begin to assemble the various "pieces" we have been considering throughout this book.

It is often quite difficult to start looking at social media and sales in a wide and comprehensive manner when the point-by-point issues have been emphasized as we have done.

It is necessary to understand everything fully, however, which is why these chapters have taken these issues one by one.

In the final chapter, however, we need to pull it all together and see how it works in your favor.

Chapter Nine

Connecting Everything Together

If you were to flip back through the pages of this book you would find many "step-by-step" instructions, tables of data, and even several versions of an ever-changing "to do" list.

What we want to do now is bring everything together into a comprehensive "Step-by-Step" Guide.

We will do that shortly, but we want to speak briefly about the proverbial "long view" and how it is going to provide you with the patience, clarity, and insight necessary to achieve success.

Taking the Long View

So what is the long view and how does it help people to achieve their goals?

Some serious clichés are associated with any discussion about the long view.

It helps you learn from your mistakes because it lets you see them from a distance.

It shows you that every road has its bumps.

It gives you a clearer perspective on the "big picture" and not the immediate problems.

You can see where all of this leads.

The long view is a way of looking at the immediate issues in front of you and putting them into the context of the future. It takes a nearly emotionless attitude to hold on to that clarity, which is not always easy to achieve.

After all, you want and need your business or company to succeed. When you take a few steps back and see that it is struggling or that your efforts are failing, you can become a bit overwrought about it.

This time calls for a bit of "disconnect," which is often only possible by putting together some organized plans or steps that can resolve some of the issues or begin to turn it around. It is highly beneficial to look at issues as a sort of checklist or on an individual basis.

Social Media Work and the Long View

Interestingly enough, when you choose some goals and work toward them, you have the option of using the long view. You can take something that you "must do" today and see how it will grow or develop over time.

For example, you want to dive right into social media marketing. We have told you, however, that it is a "learning experience."

Since we don't live in "The Matrix," we cannot just plug some program into your brain and have you fully educated in a matter of minutes. No, you have to roll up your sleeves and take the time to learn all that you need to reach the goals.

All you need to know is not an insubstantial amount of information. When you add the background knowledge needed for social media success to the amount of knowledge needed for your actual business, it can seem like a bit too much.

Just consider what we have discussed in this book—keywords, listening tools, responsiveness, all kinds of social media, developing different relationships, creating SEO content, and much more. Clearly, these are not ideas that you can just whip up right now. You have to start small and work in different levels or "phases."

So as we begin to do a Step-by-Step Guide, we'll do so in "Phases." These will roll all of the various "to do" lists and checklists that we have offered in this book into one long list of steps you will find yourself taking.

Please don't try to jump ahead. Many stories of Internet failures can point directly to "rushing into unknown territory" as the cause for disaster. Nowhere is this more common than in social media work.

You have to dedicate yourself to many hours of planning and learning before you are ready to launch a successful social media effort. You have to do a lot of research, apply that knowledge, gather data, assess the data, and more.

Fortunately, you can use this list as a sort of road map to ensure success.

Do keep in mind, however, that we have repeatedly used terms such as "we cannot tell you" or "only you can know" for a reason.

We don't know your budget, business, lifestyle, obligations, priorities, goals, and every other issue that will impact your social media work. Everything we tell you to do is going to have to be based on a few points:

- Your learning experiences
- Your intentions and needs
- Your industry conditions
- Your preferences
- Your gathered data
- Your abilities

We have also continually recommended that you seek help and support when you need it. My social media marketing firm, Sneeze It, has been mentioned a few times and is a great example of the ideal resource for all kinds of support.

How do you know when to reach out for help?

We cannot give you that answer either. We do know the most common times when professionals like yourself say "Whoa, no can do!" and then reach for the phone.

Only you will be able to say if you need some initial guidance with Phase One work or if you might need some ongoing support for your more advanced marketing.

We don't say this to discourage anyone from attempting a DIY initiative, but we do need to make you aware of the hurdles ahead.

Few business professionals understand the level of commitment necessary for a total social media campaign and what it requires to keep it moving forward.

Just getting some help with your content calendar, blog topics, and keyword discovery will be tremendously beneficial. Getting even more from social media experts is impossible to value because it can generate very small, but measurable, results or even tremendous success.

So as you go through this list of steps, keep in mind that you should never allow yourself to become overwhelmed because many experts are ready and waiting to give you the support you need.

Step-By-Step Guide to Success

Before we start going through the many steps or "phases" needed for social media marketing, we want to give you a bit of advice:

Don't Panic

In the classic book *The Hitchhiker's Guide to the Galaxy*, this phrase is imprinted on the cover of the guide to assure readers who may be hurriedly seeking a remedy to their situation. Fortunately, you don't have alien invaders or remarkable robots to worry about, but you do have a rather "epic" list of actions to complete.

This, good reader, is one of the reasons that so many people work over the long term with social media professionals. Not because the list is insurmountable or impossible, but because it is long and arduous.

A few words of caution here:

1. You have read this book, so you already know that it pays to have a basic understanding of the ways that social media marketing works.

2. Don't just coast through this list by asking someone else to tackle it. Even the world's best marketers need your assistance, input, and effort to succeed.

3. Keep in mind that the Internet is a living entity. The changes that occur on the Internet also happen in your business, which means you have to be engaged in ongoing social media marketing if you want it to keep generating good returns or results.

4. There is nothing to be afraid of.

The last one may seem a bit unnecessary, but as you have reached the end of the book, it may seem like you have quite a mountain to climb. Remember that the famous "journey of a thousand miles starts with a single step." As you begin doing each of the tasks in the lists below you will begin to see measurable effects. So without further ado, here are the lists:

Phase One

Think of this Phase as a sort of "kindergarten" period when you are learning all of the fundamentals and basics. You will master the basic vocabulary, make some essential plans and generally begin the actual "learning process" that pays you back to the extreme later on.

One major task we ask you to do from this point forward is to review your results and make adjustments to the next steps accordingly.

For example, as you move through the different phases, you have to review items such as keywords, results, comments, etc.

Using this data is very frugal and effective. So make it a habit to review everything in each phase before moving on to the next one. We also suggest that you write everything down.

Whether you start with an electronic journal, a notebook, some Excel worksheets, or a combination of all three is unimportant. What matters is that you track everything in great detail to make your reviews effective and to prevent yourself from repeating any steps unnecessarily.

1. Commit to X-number of hours of social media work each day. As we have said many times, only you can know the number of hours you are going to be willing to give to social media. You should keep two points in mind here:

   a. Most experts suggest limiting your time.

   b. The amount of time may change as your social media efforts pay off (this means more or less time may be required).

2. Learn the new sales model. Consumers are out there looking for you. Be sure you understand how to position yourself in plain sight. Understand how they look and see your information:

   a. Understand Word of Mouth

   b. Understand how User-Generated Content works

   c. Learn how both of them feature in social media

   d. Take some time to explore the most common cources of WOM

      i. Review websites

      ii. Blogs

      iii. Wikis

      iv. Social media networks

      v. Feedback forums

   e. Be sure you are comfortable in the user-controlled environment of social media

3. Commit to complete responsiveness

a. Review the amount of time you have chosen for social media work

b. Find and use all tools that will help you to remain as responsive as possible from "day one"

    i. Email alerts

    ii. Social media alerts

    iii. Strict daily schedules

    iv. Pre-written responses

    v. Automated responses

    vi. Help from social media marketing firms

4. Create a template for your ideal client

    a. What are their needs or wants?

    b. What do you have to answer them?

    c. How can you prove you are the answer?

    d. Buyer or evangelist?

    e. How old?

    f. Gender?

    g. Income?

    h. Location?

i. Educational background?

j. Interests?

k. Hobbies?

l. Groupings? Demographics often have "market segments" as part of their labeling. For instance, the 18 to 24 year old college female. Within that group however, there might be some subgroups such as "mothers," "drivers," "full time laborers," etc. Be sure you know the groupings in order to create the most accurate portrait.

5. Develop a content strategy. You may not feel that you can create any content strategy without learning more about the market. Here's the "glitch" with that way of thinking—you cannot *know* the market without running some tests and learning as much as possible. So you must begin Phase One content strategy development with the following:

    a. Establish goals. In Phase One your goals for content strategy tend to focus on making content and building networks. To do this properly, you have to first do most of the tasks below.

    b. Analyze keywords

        i. Make some well-informed guesses

        ii. Do a bit of research on the competition (see the words they use)

        iii. Use resources such as Google AdWords

        iv. Consult experts

v. Don't ignore any long tail options

c. Harvest demographics (because you have already made a client template, you have a lot of this information. Now also seek it for your industry, product, service, etc.):

i. Look for infographics

ii. Seek out your industry statistics

iii. Learn about the preferred social media for your audience

d. Define yourself

i. B2B or B2C? Maybe C2C?

ii. Local or broad based? Will you target a local audience or the entire web?

e. Summarize your business. Be sure you can summarize your business in about 40 words or less. Consider using

i. Specific product

ii. Brand name

iii. Type of industry

iv. Descriptive words for products

v. Consumer "slang"

f. Discover where you audience "hangs out" in social networks. You cannot strategize without knowing which of the social media your audience prefers. Find this by doing the following:

i. Listening

1. Social mesdia

2. RSS subscriptions

3. Alerts from search engines and social media for specific terms, etc.

ii. Discovering what is being said. Is it all relatively positive? Is the industry viewed unfavorably? What is the general "word on the street"?

iii. Starting to learn the language of the audience. Do they use the words you use or do they have an entirely separate set of terms?

6. Ask yourself the most useful questions:

a. What does the audience want to talk about?

b. Where will the most conversations take place?

c. How can you measure the conversations you are going to have?

7. Craft an initial message that you will give away. Be sure that this message

a. Is not a sales message in any way

b. Contains information useful to your audience

c. Is easily shared

d. Contains the most likely keywords based on your research

8. Test the message by

a. Creating a way of tracking results

b. Sending to those who fit the client template and any sub-group information

c. Using one or two sites for initial social media efforts based on your findings

d. Tracking information you receive about your audience, keywords, and industry from response

9. Assess and analyze the findings

10. Use what you have learned to start much more targeted networking

Phase Two

By now, you are at the point where you are starting to get a feel for social media marketing. You see where your audience is hanging out, you are learning the "lingo," and you are beginning to understand how to speak to them directly without also trying to make the sale.

Let's consider that initial "sub-set" of "to do" items we mentioned all of the way back in Chapter Two:

1. *Getting the attention of your market*

2. *Getting them to respect you and your knowledge*

3. *Making them like the product*

4. *Keeping the interaction going*

5. *Making ongoing sales*

Now *is the time when you are going to be able to seriously consider the best ways to do such tasks because you have started to really develop a good foundation. Right now you have created some targeted messages, so that is where we begin the next phase "to do" list.*

1. Continue targeted messaging

2. Expand your audience in the one or two social media networks you have already been using by

   a. Friending, following, liking, etc. others in your field and your possible audience

   b. Ensuring that most new traffic is "qualified"

   c. Using your existing contact lists in social media

   d. Branding your pages by

      i. Creating a YouTube channel

      ii. Using a custom Twitter background

      iii. Building a Facebook landing page

      iv. Making a detailed LinkedIn profile

3. Establish credibility by

    a. Creating a blog

    b. Enhancing the blog to ensure interaction and traffic by

        i. Embedding links about it on social media

        ii. Filling the blog with keywords and metadata

        iii. Using video and audio content in the blogs

        iv. Seeking to do SEO through the blog and associated activities

4. Generate top of the line content, such as

    a. SEO blogs and traditional blog content

    b. SEO articles and regular articles posted to social media platforms and article directories

    c. Wall posts on Facebook

    d. Interactions on Facebook

    e. Tweets

    f. Twitter interactions

    g. Google+ posts

    h. Google+ interactions

    i. Profiles on sites such as LinkedIn

j. Pinterest Boards

k. Photos (including those on Flickr)

l. YouTube videos

m. Tags, titles, and identifying labels on all content listed above

5. Learn about SEO and begin to consider

a. Page optimization

b. Links

c. Social media interaction

6. Make a new content calendar that is focused on lead generation

By this point we have reached only item #2 on that list of "sub-set" goals. You have grabbed the attention of your audience or market and have started showing them that you are credible and respectable. It is time, however, to stop for a bit and look at what you have accomplished and where you are headed.

Why? We are about to move into Phase Three, which is about lead generation and audience retention. These are a bit more complex and require that you have reviewed your successes and failures to maximize your time and the return on any effort expended.

Phase Three

If you are doing those reviews we suggested, you have really honed and refined your client template, have discovered the right key-

words and blog topics, and are learning the best ways of speaking to your market through social media.

Now you can safely bump activities up a bit and begin expanding the size of the audience and branching out into overlapping areas of interest.

1. Review the discussion on ROI in Chapter Six, and make some preliminary choices for measuring your results

2. Focus on lead generation through

    a. SEO content

    b. Blogging

    c. Finding common interest groups on all social media sites

    d. Generating content relevant to your lead-generation efforts

    e. Advertising

3. Focus on retention through

    a. Maximizing content discovery

    b. Posting new content often

    c. Enabling the sharing of content

    d. Creating social thank you pages

    e. Prolonging the shelf life of social media links

f. Keeping in touch

g. Networking

h. Avoiding hard sales

i. Creating an "expert" reputation

j. Giving away valuable materials

k. Interacting to the fullest extent

l. Developing a good "voice" in your messages and communication

m. Positioning yourself in the best "view" to your audience

4. Create buzz opportunities on all social media and website pages, including

    a. Sending them offsite

    b. Offering games and contests

    c. Using widgets

    d. Expanding on blogs via videos, eBooks, etc.

    e. Avoiding any broadcasting and focusing on generating positive attention and interest.

    f. Following "winning" examples. Remember that we talked about maximizing the shelf lives of your social media posts by creating multiple "levels" of contact. Here are some excellent examples:

i. Example One:

1. Create a blog, and send out alerts to all social media pages when a new entry is posted.

2. Create video content for the blog and use the same social media channels to announce the video at a later date.

3. Create downloadable content relating to the blog and/or video and again post alerts.

4. Find a guest blogger to write a partner blog or commentary, and use social media to comment on it, thank the blogger, etc.

ii. Example Two:

1. Create an online gathering such as a podcast, seminar, event, etc. Invite participants through the blog, social media, and website.

2. After the event, thank the presenters through social media pages and embed links to their portion of the event.

iii. Example Three:

1. Create a contest on each of the social media sites. Make the contests relevant to the nature of the network (images for Pinterest, videos for YouTube, text for social media, etc.)

2. Announce the contest through social media, the blog, and the website.

3. Use an email list to alert the audience about the contest

4. Announce winners and links to their "entries" (if possible) through social media

iv. Example Four:

1. Create a custom community on each of your social networks

2. Use them to host games, contests, polls, forums, etc.

3. Market them through all of your social media, blogs, and websites.

4. Use what occurs in the community to steer your marketing efforts

5. Focus on conversion by

a. Listening and being responsive by

i. Using listening tools and responding to each share, tweet, etc.

ii. Using customer posts, feedback, etc. to discover new subject matter for material and new keywords, etc.

iii. Using the content calendar as a basis for regular activity

    iv. Returning any social media favors by being a responder

b. Creating a call to action. Remember that these can be

    i. Links in blogs or on social media

    ii. Clear instructions to "buy now"

    iii. Subscription buttons

    iv. Links to "learn more," accept a free offer, etc.

    v. Passive or active requests

    vi. Asking the right questions:

        1. Why should they follow the call?

        2. What do they get from it?

        3. Am I using active language?

        4. Is it in plain sight?

c. Communicating offline when necessary

Phase Four

What has it cost you? You have gotten their attention, ensured that your audience is seeing you as a credible and valid entity, and encouraged them to take action, but what has it brought in terms of a return? Yes, we have reached the point where the ROI has to be calculated.

Now is the time to start to consider some serious measurements. Though you have already been tracking items such as keywords and responses, you have to roll it all into a financial equation, too.

What did the effort, energy, time, and thought cost versus the amount you earned? Did you earn actual dollars? Was that even the goal? Perhaps you are going to have to consider the SROI?

We won't lie to you. Calculating ROI is a moment when a lot of people sigh heavily and decide that they will seek some help. It is very challenging to tackle all of your social media tasks without losing track of the effort of financial costs. It is also a bit of a challenge to know if you even should be continuing with specific tasks.

Thus, your next Phase begins with the following:

1. Calculate ROI by using such tools as
    a. Analytics
        i. Tracking software
        ii. Social media monitoring software to know who is talking about your content
        iii. Analytical tools available online
    b. Local results
    c. Failures
    d. Responses to Calls to Action
2. Set measurable goals for ROI in order to test and assess (be sure to pair items that can overlap or work together)

3. Choose good data collection methods such as the use of Excel or specialized software, and then track

    a. Goals

    b. Methods used to meet goals

    c. Numbers associated with social media reaction (i.e., number of likes, shares, tweets, etc.)

    d. Website data resulting from social media

    e. Copies of all text, comments, etc.

    f. Total number of hours spent on effort

    g. Share of voice

    h. Sentiment

4. Assess the results of social media and the ROI information by asking

    a. Did I reach the goal I set out to reach?

    b. What did it cost me financially?

    c. How much time did it honestly demand?

    d. Was it very challenging in terms of effort and knowledge?

    e. Do I sincerely believe it was a worthwhile "investment"?

5. Follow up by

a. Deciding on your priority

   i. More traffic

   ii. Maintain current traffic and more sales?

b. Determining your traffic's intent by

   i. Using data to see where traffic dropped

   ii. Using data to see if any flaws are in the process

   iii. Discovering what your audience is seeking by following their steps and preferences

   iv. Optimizing to meet their intent through the use of further data analysis. This analysis can be done by paying attention to your competition and their conversion rates but is something that most will do with the support of a social media marketing professional.

   v. Improving value of content to get attention, retain attention, and motivate audience through the use of

      1. Videos/podcasts

      2. Visuals

      3. PPC

      4. Guest blogs

Phase Five

What are the results up to this point? Are you becoming aware of the major sources for traffic to your site? Have you found that you are not getting the results you anticipated? If you answered yes, or even if you didn't, you should direct some time to your reputation and the amount of trust you are building in your audience.

Why? Trust and a good reputation can really make the difference between mediocre to poor results and results that are off the charts. Remember that you are selling in the online model, which is a tough environment for consumers.

You can overcome the challenges to the usual one-on-one model by following the steps below.

1. Build trust through

    a. Responsiveness

    b. Creating a good impression

    c. Performing an introductory dialogue

    d. Listening and responding

    e. Following up accordingly with a thank you and free materials or through "calls to action" such as trackable social media buttons to use

    f. *Not* selling

    g. Showing a readiness to solve problems

    h. Being responsible for good and bad social media information

    i. Helping customers without "payback"

j. Showing a long term interest

2. Use media in a hierarchal way: video, audio, social media with imagery, text alone

3. Develop allied relationships

4. Ask for feedback when possible and gather large quantities of it

5. Protect the reputation by

    a. Learning how to handle threats to the reputation

    b. Making video apologies

    c. Offering well-structured responses and/or apologies that

        i. Occur immediately

        ii. Work as an "in person" apology

        iii. Rely on the person in charge to convey the message

        iv. Convey a sense of responsibility

        v. Express ownership of the issue

        vi. Let you say aloud what you are apologizing for

        vii. Help to show your true emotional response

        viii. Allow you a forum for indicating how you will remedy the issue

   d. Knowing how to use social media to recover a tarnished reputation by

      i. Re-engaging the audience

      ii. Rewarding the audience for its faith

      iii. Encouraging a reassessment of the brand/business/etc.

   e. Making social media thank yous/acknowledgements that include

      i. Landing pages

      ii. Videos

      iii. Notifications

6. Manage social media reputation to

   a. Enhance your online presence

   b. Counteract negativity against your firm or your industry

   c. Have a system for responding to negative comments or feedback in a professional way

   d. Give you the best image available

   e. Use as a form of outreach

7. Have "no fail" techniques for true social media problems, including

a. Retaining comments

b. Leaving them public

c. Addressing them instantly

d. Being ready with answers

e. Controlling the tone of any discussions

f. Getting help when needed

g. Knowing when to stop interacting

h. Monitoring the fallout

8. Build a "tribe." Apart from an audience, you need advocates and likeminded people all over your social media pages. To do this you should

   a. Look at the existing audience and client template to determine the characteristics of a good "tribal" member

   b. Determine the keywords that apply to your desired tribal model

   c. Seek groups that already meet these requirements in all social media sites, and connect with them

   d. Understand that a tribal member takes you at face value and will

      i. Follow you

      ii. Help spread the word about you

iii. Nurture the strength of your business

iv. Help you to constantly refine and clarify your "message"

v. Generally give you an enhanced social media presence

e. Return the favor by creating a pleasant tribal culture that allows everyone to

i. Give feedback and opinions

ii. Interact freely

iii. Encourage one another

iv. Participate in regular events

f. Decide if you want tribal members or if brand evangelists are a wiser option.

9. Gather brand evangelists. Brand evangelists will not be as interactive with one another as a tribe but will still spread the word about you without any need for reward. They use

a. WOM

b. Conversational marketing

c. Premium content supplied by you, including

i. SEO-rich content

ii. Multimedia materials

iii. Ongoing and frequently updated materials

iv. Contests, etc.

10. Encourage evangelism by employing the following social media tactics

    a. Bowing

    b. Check-ins

    c. Hallmarking

    d. Huddling

    e. Must Reads

    f. Mysteries

    g. News Flashes

    h. Images

    i. Pursuing them relentlessly, but without sales pressure

    j. Promoting them

    k. Taking actions offline

11. Conduct an SR`OI on them to be sure they are generating enough rewards for the effort by

    a. Finding the themes of shared materials

    b. Generating campaigns around those themes

c. Engaging the most likely evangelists

d. Tracking their participation and results

e. Setting measurable goals for the campaign

f. Determining if the evangelists and/or materials generated the desired results

PHEW! That is a tremendous amount "to do," and the sooner you get started the better. Just keep in mind that we have broken everything out into manageable bits and pieces. This ensures that you don't get overwhelmed and that you can even divide larger tasks up into individual tasks.

For example, why not look at Phase One and do only items one and two this week? There should never be a "rush" to get these tasks done. Yes, your business needs to make a profit, but you can only guarantee good results with social media when you take the time to really build a solid foundation.

Never be afraid to ask for some help because this is very tough work. Experts are out there, and we are ready to roll up our sleeves and help you tackle the largest and smallest issues. Just use the Phases and steps above to see where you need to go.

We wish you the best of luck and know that soon you will wonder how you ever did any business without the availability of social media marketing options, sneezing, and the Internet!

Resources

Glossary

Here you will find definitions of the most common terms associated with your social media work. We have used all of these phrases and words in the text but feel that you will benefit from having a handy reference when you begin doing some of your initial and ongoing social media work.

These terms are also very useful to know when you are speaking with social media marketing professionals, and knowing their meanings will make you look like a real pro!

- **Active Listening.** Taking in all that is being said and formulating questions based on interest in what is heard. Not allowing yourself to be distracted by other thoughts and being able to fully understand all that is said.
- **Algorithm.** Mathematical rules for solving a problem in a finite number of steps. Search engines operate by using algorithms.
- **App.** An application that performs a specific function on your computer or handheld device.

- **Black Hat SEO.** A relatively generic term used for unethical or deceptive search engine optimization techniques. This includes spam, cloaking, or violating search engine rules in any way, such as keyword stuffing or copying and pasting content. When any search engine discovers a site engaging in black hat SEO it will remove it from its index.
- **Blog**. An online journal that is updated on a regular basis with entries that appear in reverse chronological order. Blogs can be about any subject. They typically contain comments by other readers, links to other sites, URLs, embedded video content, images, and more.
- **Branding.** Being sure that a website or social media page is clearly marked with the identity of a specific product, service, or business.
- **Campaign.** A set of coordinated marketing messages, delivered at intervals, with a specific goal, such as boosting traffic or increasing sales of a product.
- **Content Strategy.** Developing a calendar by which you will release your online content. This calendar is created only after clear goals have been established; keywords identified; and the choice of video, text, audio, or multimedia content has been made.
- **Crowd Sourcing.** Refers to harnessing the skills and enthusiasm of those outside an organization who are prepared to volunteer their time contributing content or skills and solving problems. Another term for evangelism.
- **Demographic.** The study of, or information about, people's lifestyles, habits, population movements, spending, age, social grade, employment, etc.
- **EBooks.** An electronic version of a traditional printed book that can be downloaded from the Internet and read on your computer or handheld device. Something as simple as a PDF document can be considered an eBook.
- **Embedding.** The act of adding code to a website so that a video or photo can be displayed while it's being hosted at

another site. Many users now watch embedded YouTube videos or see Flickr photos on blogs and websites rather than on the originating site.

- **Facebook.** The most popular social networking site in the world, with more than 955 million active users. Users' timeline streams can now be seen on a wide range of applications and devices.
- **Feed.** A web feed or RSS feed provides users with frequently updated content. Content distributors syndicate a web feed, enabling users to subscribe to a site's latest content. By using a newsreader to subscribe to a feed, you can read the latest posts or watch the newest videos.
- **Flickr.** The world's top photo-sharing and hosting site.
- **Geotagging.** The process of adding location-based metadata to media such as photos, video, or online maps.
- **Google AdWords.** Google's trademarked name of its PPC advertisement system.
- **Hashtag.** A community-driven method for adding additional context to tweets. They are added to Twitter posts by prefixing a word with a hash symbol (or number sign). Twitter users use a hashtag to aggregate, organize, track, and discover relevant posts.
- **Hosting.** A blog, video, or podcast needs a hosting service before it can appear online. Companies sometimes host their blogs on their own servers, but a better approach for video or audio is to use a host such as YouTube.
- **Long tail keyword.** A keyword with three or more terms. More of a phrase, it is meant to really hone and sharpen the results. It is also used for geographically based searches.
- **Metadata.** Refers to information (including titles, descriptions, tags, and captions) that describes a media item such as a video, photo, or blog post.
- **Needs Assessment.** A marketing tactic that takes into consideration all possible factors that may drive a consumer to make a specific purchase.

- **Newsreader.** Sometimes called a feed reader, RSS reader, or news aggregator, a newsreader gathers the news from multiple blogs or news sites via RSS feeds.
- **Open media.** Video, audio, text and other media that can be freely shared, often by using creative commons or GPL licenses.
- **Organic SEO.** The process of using the most accepted practices or guidelines that Google, Yahoo, and Bing provide. This ensures that a website can receive higher search engine rankings based on its content, rather than relying on paid advertising, dubious tactics, or manipulation of web page codes or external links to achieve higher search engine rankings.
- **Paid search marketing.** Paid ads for a business or service on a search engine results page (SERP). The advertiser pays the search engine only if the visitor clicks on the PPC (pay per click) ad.
- **Permalink.** A direct link to a blog entry that does not change.
- **Pinterest.** A pinboard style photo-sharing social media site that allows users to create and manage theme-based image collections such as events, interests, hobbies, and more.
- **Podcast.** A digital file (usually audio but sometimes video) made available for download to a portable device or personal computer. Podcasts use a feed to which users subscribe and which alerts them when a new audio clip is published online.
- **RSS**. Web standard for the delivery of content—blog entries, news stories, headlines, images, video. RSS stands for Really Simple Syndication. All blogs, podcasts, and video blogs contain an RSS feed, which lets users subscribe to content automatically and read or listen to the material. Most people use an RSS reader, or news aggregator, to monitor updates.

- **Screencast.** Video that captures what takes place on a computer screen, usually accompanied by narration. Often created to explain a "how to," but it can be any piece of video that pulls together images or visuals.
- **Search engine marketing.** Online tactics that, combined with SEO, help to attract relevant customers. Will also generate brand awareness and build trust. Its goal is to increase a website's visibility through the use of PPC ads and paid inclusion.
- **Search engine optimization (SEO).** Process of enhancing a website to give it the best chance of appearing near the top of search engine rankings. It is a complete Internet marketing strategy and uses the infrastructure of search engines to reach goals. Optimization involves editing content, finding the high-traffic keywords, and designing the site for easy reading by web "bots."
- **Social bookmarking.** Users store lists of personally interesting Internet resources and usually make these lists publicly accessible to like-minded searchers. They are tools by which users locate, share, store, organize, and manage bookmarks of web pages.
- **Social Influence Marketing.** Engaging with social media and social influencers to achieve the marketing and business needs of an organization.
- **Social media.** User-created text, video, audio, or multimedia that are shared on a social website, such as a blog, forum, podcast, wiki, review site, or video hosting site. Also, any online technology that lets people publish, exchange, and share content online.
- **Social networking.** Socializing in an online community. Social networks such as Facebook, LinkedIn, MySpace, or Google+ allow users to create a profile, add friends, communicate with other members, and add all kinds of media.

- **Social return on investment.** SROI refers to the non-financial returns sought by a social entrepreneur.
- **Streaming media.** Podcasts or video available for download; streaming media is most often video or audio that can be watched or listened to online but not stored permanently.
- **Tags.** Keywords added to a blog post, photo, or video to help web bots, search engines, and visitors find related topics or media. Tags work through regular browsing or can be relevant to search engines.
- **Tweet.** An original post on Twitter. RT stands for retweet: users add RT in a tweet if they are reposting something from another person's tweet.
- **Twitter.** A leading social network that lets members post updates of no more than 140 characters.
- **User-generated content.** All forms of user-created materials including blog posts, reviews, podcasts, videos, comments, and more.
- **Video blog (vlog).** Blog that contains video entries, also known as video podcasting, vodcasting, or vlogging.
- **Web 2.0.** Concept that takes the network as a platform for information sharing, interoperability, user-centered design, and collaboration on the World Wide Web.
- **Web analytics.** Measurement, collection, analysis, and reporting of Internet data with the intent of using it to understand visitors to a website.
- **Webcasting.** Using the web to deliver live or delayed versions of audio or video broadcasts.
- **Webinar.** A presentation, lecture, workshop, or seminar that is transmitted over the web.
- **Widget.** A small block of content, displayed with a specific purpose, such as providing news, which is constantly updating itself (typically via RSS). Widgets add dynamic content to a site or blog.

- **Wikis.** A web site developed collaboratively by a community of users, allowing any user to add and edit content.
- **Word-of-mouth marketing (WOM).** An umbrella term for techniques used to engage more customers. It works by building relationships with "evangelists" through WOM and encouraging people to become enthusiastic about a product or service. It will drive sales through conversations.
- **YouTube.** The world's most popular video-hosting site.

www.ingramcontent.com/pod-product-compliance
Lightning Source LLC
Chambersburg PA
CBHW061505180526
45171CB00001B/42
9781479370405